To

*Jill and Norman Franklin*

*The modern movement is dead; long live the modern movement.*

# PREFACE

This book is a modern theory of architecture, not a theory of 'modern' architecture. It is *modern* in the sense that it deals with awareness of architecture in the present time: it would be outrageous to claim that it is original. Architecture has existed for thousands of years and is comparable in quality across the centuries, but there seems to be a need for a way of thinking about architecture, past and present, which is tuned to the condition of our time. We can look at things in fresh ways but we are dealing with a subject which is age-old and in which it is doubtful whether we can excel our ancestors.

This book is not a history, but it must sometimes allude to the past and presume some knowledge of architectural history in the reader. It is not a guide to practice nor a handbook on the techniques of design. What we require of a Theory of Architecture is that it should be *a basis for discussing architecture as such*, as a phenomenon generated by mankind, in a way which will make us aware of architectural values and enable us to explore them creatively both in the design and the enjoyment of architecture.

This is not a path leading to a finite destination: it is a journey towards a prospect.

*Throughout this book the main argument is presented in the left-hand column of the text. The right-hand column is used for notes, diagrams, illustrations and glosses upon the text.*

# ACKNOWLEDGMENTS

I am indebted to many people who have helped with this book, directly or indirectly, over a long period, and recently to my colleagues David Saile and Charles Fox for stimulating discussion of the first formulation of my ideas; to NEG at Leeds Polytechnic and the audience at Leeds School of Architecture which listened to and commented upon an early version; to my tutorial group at Newcastle School of Architecture; to Donald Langmead of Adelaide School of Architecture for many stimulating discussions in the course of his important work on folk architecture; to Hentie Louw for enlightening conversations and an insight into his remarkable understanding of the origins of renaissance architecture; to my son Christopher for formative discussions about economics; to Dr. P.W. Kent, Master of Van Mildert College, Durham, and the late Professor Gilbert Ryle, whose book, *Contemporary Aspects of Philosophy*, based upon the 1975 conference at Christ Church College Oxford, I sub-edited while I was writing *A Modern Theory of Architecture*, with considerable effect upon my own thinking; to Richard Seed with whose on-going work on architectural aesthetics I have had the privilege of being associated as supervisor for his doctorate; to Frank Jenkins (founder of the Society of Architectural Historians of Great Britain) over many years, but recently for his careful reading and comments on the final draft; to Professor Ralph Crowe also for reading and commenting upon the typescript; to the publishers' anonymous reader for his encouragement and the imposition of a stricter discipline; and finally, and most gratefully, to Norman Franklin for having the faith to publish a new book on the theory of architecture in these difficult times.

*And in production to Carol Gardiner for editing and Beryl Burke for typing and proof-correction.*

*Architectural theory in the west has a long pedigree going back, through Vitruvius to the ancient Greeks and, by implication, to Egypt and Mesopotamia. The principal works which a serious student of the history of a theoretical approach to the study of architecture should begin by reading are as follows. Vitruvius,* De Architectura *(1st century BC); Alberti,* De Re Aedificatoria *(Florence, 1485); Philibert de l'Orme,* L'Architecture *(Paris 1567); M-A. Laugier,* Essai sur l'Architecture *(Paris 1752); David Hume, Essay,* On the Standard of Taste *(London 1742); John Ruskin,* The Seven Lamps of Architecture *(London 1849); Julien Guadet,* Eléments et Theorie de l'Architecture *(Paris 1904); Le Corbusier,* Vers une Architecture *(Paris 1923); Niels Luning Prak,* The Language of Architecture *(The Hague 1968).*

*These are all seminal books. There are many others which derive from them, e.g.* The Four Books of Architecture *by Andrea Palladio which derives from Vitruvius and Alberti.*

# CONTENTS

# INTRODUCTION

Many friends, whose opinions I respect, have told me that it is impossible to write a modern theory of architecture, and yet there has never been a greater need for architects to bridge the widening gap of understanding between them and the public. To build a bridge one must explain the values of architecture to the public, but unless architects themselves can have a coherent system of belief about architecture, understanding by the public may be impossible.

At the present time most architects seem to settle for a belief in developing what they call a 'personal philosophy' of architecture; but if this is merely personal to them and not expressible in terms which can be generally understood, the end product is a demand, by the architect, to be regarded and respected as an autonomous artist, whose work subscribes to no general principles and can only be explained in terms of the architect's own belief in its value. For the rare genius this may be justified but for the thousands of ordinary architects it is not.

The modern movement of the inter-war and post-second-world-war periods was much more diverse than many of its protagonists were prepared to admit, and there was a closing of the ranks—the modernists against the rest. This was so effective as to give some substance to the claim that there should be *one* architecture for the whole world. Though many of the best modernistic architects were refugees from political totalitarianism, they propagated an intolerant and totalitarian architecture which was a reflection of the rigid intolerances of the age.

'Modern' architecture was anti-stylistic, claimed not to be a style, and yet it has become one and, as with all styles, fashion has operated first to popularise and then reject it. We have reached a point where architects practise in a style which seems to be undefinable on any theoretical basis but rests upon the use of forms and conventions which are increasingly distasteful to the public.

What we seem to need now is a basis for talking and thinking about architecture which does not assume that every architect, and indeed every second-year student of architecture, is a budding or blossoming Brunelleschi, Sinan, François Mansart, Wren, or Frank Lloyd Wright. Such people occur one or two to a century and all those I have named succeeded to cumulative experiences of architecture which they were able to gather and project into the future.

A major obstacle to the development of a modern theory is that architects expect it to be in the form of the only theoretical consideration of architecture which has stood the

*Modern societies offer to the 'creative minority' increased opportunities in science, industry and (beguilingly) in administration. It is less likely now than five hundred years ago that outstanding talents will be turned towards the arts, including architecture. It is socially important that architecture should should compete effectively for such talents.*

*'Modern' architecture reflects an age of faith in simplistic or 'total' solutions to the social problems of mankind: a faith in systems. It also reflects belief among architects in their dictatorial autonomy. Totalitarian seems to be the best adjective to describe the movement and this may become its title in history.*

test of time, namely *De Architectura* by Vitruvius. This was up-dated in the fifteenth century by Alberti to form the theoretical basis of renaissance architecture. Modern architects rightly see that modern architecture cannot be explained in this way, but there is no other model. We have to start afresh.

This book does not presume to tell architects of genius how they should design. It recognises that building is a fundamental necessity for mankind: people and industries must be housed; but there is a phenomenon, revealed throughout human history, which we call *architecture*. This can turn a hut, a bridge, a factory, an office, a shop, a place of worship, into something more than it is of its own right. This is architecture—*significant building*.

*Architecture is* significant *building.*

The subject is complex. This book will not be an argument in the old, conventional form of two-value logic towards a conclusion. It rejects, from the outset, the specious simplicity of critical-path analysis. It recognises that understanding must be built up like a mosaic. The form of the book is a mosaic in which a multitude of parts are interrelated. The first section is a consideration; the second a body of suggestions based upon the study of elements which can only be isolated for purposes of consideration but which in reality are parts of a living whole, dependent for their nature upon their relatedness. The reader is invited to study this book as a cumulative experience of the nature of architecture.

*cf.* Belnap D., How A Computer Should Think, *in Ryle, G.* Contemporary Aspects of Philosophy *(Stocksfield 1976).*

PART I

# PART I

# CONSIDERATION

## 1. KINDS OF ARCHITECTURE

It is necessary for man to build. Even the simplest building involves a series of decisions. To some extent decisions may be predetermined by tradition, by the builder's knowledge of the right way to do things according to the custom of his people. On this basis a people develops a characteristic architecture. We call this *folk architecture*.

Even a bird's nest requires special decisions to be made by the builder; the selection of the site and necessary adaptations of the normal design to make it buildable on that site. Thereafter, it seems, birds adhere to the formula which is characteristic of their species.

The buildings of men, being larger and more complex, give rise to a greater number of unique decisions. Man is an unusually adaptable animal. He is capable of evolving culturally, through cumulative experience of adaptation and successive creative decisions. Decisions may be made collectively—by voting for example—but ideas occur in a single mind from which they may be communicated.

In the process of building a man may make decisions which derive from his own ideas. His ideas and therefore in a sense, his *self*, seem to be embodied in the building—in the *design*.

The architecture of a folk is evolved and modified by ideas and imitation. Folk architecture is capable of diversity and differentiation. A hundred Swiss chalets may look alike and all be different, just as a hundred people are superficially alike but all different. Architecture begins with creative decisions by the builder and differentiations which he associates with himself.

But some creative decisions are successful and some are not. We tend to say some are *good* and some are *bad* but this is mistaken because they are not *moral* decisions. They are *expedient* decisions and success or failure depends upon a host of external factors; social, structural, climatic, cultural and economic. Of these the cultural factor may be the most important in that it embodies what is acceptable to the community.

Man discovered that over and above satisfying his functional needs the decisions he made in designing a building created a

*Folk architecture—the architecture of people—is the original architecture but the need of man to use building to express communal feeling leads to spiritual and monumental architecture at a very primitive stage of development and a primitive subjugation of humane to monumental and spiritual architecture. (See below).*
*Inhumanity is extremely primitive. Men had to learn to be humane and the process continues.*

cf. Rappoport, A. House Form and Culture (London 1969).

relationship between him and the building, giving it meaning. Architecture is building with which people have identified themselves, giving it significance.

In folk architecture significance is given to the individual as a member of the community—the folk. Custom predominates and design is within the context of custom; but folk architecture is design by people for people in the context of a community of people. It is intelligible and congenial just as a dialect is.

In the older countries of the world it can still be seen that folk architecture is localised, often to a single valley or a few square miles of plain. The reasons for this are sometimes apparent. They are often cultural and ethnic. Folk architecture is generally the architecture of small communities.

The grouping of villages into larger organisations, with the emergence of towns and cities, creates new architectural needs which cannot be satisfied entirely by folk architecture. A new kind of man is required, the architect.

*The emergence of the Architect.*

It is apparent that different villages have different architecture and each is significant of its own locality and people. The idea of significance becomes generalised; it is seen as a property which architecture has. A process of synthesis then begins in the minds of architects—they see folk architecture as a way of designing and think of themselves as designing 'in the vernacular'. Vernacular is really a linguistic term, but it is transferred to architecture: an architect designs in the built equivalent of the common way of speech, be it local, as in a dialect, or national, as in the differences between the Welsh, Scottish, Irish or American ways of speaking English or the Provencal, Norman, Auvergnat or Québec ways of speaking French. Vernacular architecture uses the design skills of architects to *develop* folk architecture.

*A distinction is necessary between folk and vernacular architecture. The architect who uses folk traditions as a basis for design is designing in the vernacular.*

From early times men have venerated natural objects such as trees, caves, standing stones or conical hills. They have made mounds and set up stones and tree trunks, giving them religious and magical significance. They have set up altars and made buildings to house the paraphernalia of sacrifice or worship. They have proceeded to build temples signifying not only themselves and their own aspirations but also the power and attributes of a spirit or deity. Much early religion was functional. It was intended to achieve beneficial results: fertility, rain, sunshine, the rotation of the seasons. Significance and function were determined by priests who claimed to be expert in functionally correct and spiritually significant building. This architecture, concerned with man's relationship to spiritual powers, was capable of development to high levels of sophistication. It was also capable of different levels of interpretation, as in the case of the Parthenon, which could be seen as a votive offering to a capricious patron goddess or as the outward symbol of the city's awareness of its corporate existence.

*Spiritual architecture* is significant and symbolic of man's relation to unseen powers which may be gods, spirits, forces of nature, awarenesses, ideas, ideologies or concepts. The essence of *spiritual architecture* is that it is intended to have *meaning* and this is its *primary* function.

*The idea of functionalism needs to include the function of expressing meaning.*

The phenomenon of death is awe-inspiring, its circumstances often pathetic, the belief in a soul persistent and the desire for commemoration deeply rooted. The marking of a grave is the beginning of *monumental architecture*. The purpose is to commemorate and honour. The simplest, indeed the inevitable form is a mound which the emphasis appropriate to a mighty king elevates into the pyramid and elaborates into the mausoleum. Already in ancient Egypt men are building tombs during their lifetimes to commemorate them in death. The idea of the monument as a dignification of the dead is extended into life. Monuments are erected in honour of the living to outlast their bodily existence. The intention to remember, the complimentary status-symbol, gives monumental architecture an honorific role among the living, and the association with death is tactfully played down until it is almost forgotten.

*A simple interment produces a temporary mound. The monument is intended to perpetuate what nature absorbs and obliterates.*

Monumental architecture is honorific in its significance and is extended from persons to institutions, to governments, corporations and banks. Death and religion being closely associated in the minds of men, the distinction between monumental and spiritual architecture is often blurred. There is some merging of intention and significance but there is an original difference. Spiritual architecture is related to non-corporeal things, monumental architecture to people and it is important to keep this distinction in mind.

Utilitarian building takes as many forms as there are purposes to be served, but in the past it has generally not been regarded as architecture, the reason being that it was simply serving a purpose without having any other significance. Castles or city walls might be given monumental or spiritual additions, such as elaborated gateways intended to impress the visitor and express the importance and pride of the inhabitants. Indeed almost any building could be taken out of the utility class by giving it significance other than its inherent function, but the design then lost its utilitarian character and assumed the garb of another kind of architecture. Frequently this was monumental as in the great Thermae of ancient Rome or the stables of a pretentious mansion.

*Until recently the patrons of architecture have generally been priests or potentates. The homes and work-places of the common people have not been thought of as architecture. The nineteenth century brought a vulgarisation of architecture. Vulgar means 'of the common people' and by old standards this meant vile and contemptible. If we live in the age of enfranchisement of the common man, with mass education and some approximation to equality of opportunity, we should pay particular homage to the architecture of the nineteenth century as the first vulgar architecture.*

*Snobbery is the occupational disease of art historians who enjoy the role of posthumous vicarious patron! Indeed all historians of every political complexion are liable to identify with the rulers rather than the ruled.*

8

With the Industrial Revolution and the development of technology, manufacture and commerce in manufactured goods became the basis of a way of life. The devices of spiritual and monumental architecture were deployed for a time in mitigation of utilitarian design until materialism came of age and the expression of material function became a significant architectural objective in its own right. Utilitarian building became *utilitarian architecture*.

There are now five kinds of architecture; *folk, vernacular, spiritual, monumental* and *utilitarian*. These kinds may merge, both in the programme and in the solution but fundamentally they are different, require different skills and different criteria of criticism. Much of the confusion in modern architectural thinking has arisen from failure to recognise that there are different kinds of architecture.

*Folk architecture* is the natural domestic architecture of a people. If they migrate they commonly take it with them, even in defiance of climate, but practicality operates over a period of time to adapt the original forms to new conditions, frequently producing a new folk style derived from the old. The characteristics of folk architecture extend to simple communal buildings such as churches, workshops, warehouses and barns. Originality in the design of architectural form is minimal and differentiation is mainly a matter of building type, detail and craftsmanship in decoration. Folk architecture is concerned with the comfort and convenience of its inhabitants, congeniality being the prerequisite of comfort.

*Vernacular architecture* is a generalised way of design derived from folk architecture. It may be seen as the development of the 'natural' architecture of a region which is definable in terms of climate, culture and materials. Of its own nature, however, vernacular architecture is limited to that which can properly be expressed 'in the vernacular'. It can be used for spiritual, monumental and utility buildings but limits of propriety are set by taste and judgment. *Scale* is a crucial factor. Vernacular architecture is congenial to people and sympathetic to environment. It is for loving rather than admiration.

*Spiritual architecture* is designed towards spiritual or notional clients, humans being agents for them. The inspiration of something over and above the human begetter of the building has led to economic provision beyond the ordinary and the creation of the majority of the world's most admired buildings. It is a germane paradox that the greatest buildings have been

*It is interesting that battlements acquired and retained, long after they had become functionally obsolete, an honorific significance because they were a symbol of social status. This has persisted into one of the mannerisms of 'modern' architecture.*

*It requires the extreme sophistication of self-negation for the modern kind of architect to design in the folk tradition. C.F.A. Voysey was one who achieved this and, despite his aristocratic connections, so did Sir Edwin Lutyens.*

*Many people, e.g. St Bernard of Clairvaux, have distrusted architecture as a medium of spiritual expression. The first Quaker, George Fox, called church buildings 'steeple houses' and insisted that the Church was people, not buildings.*

produced when it would have been an impiety to count the cost, but lavish expenditure in itself has produced some of the worst buildings in the world. This suggests to us that motivation and significance are crucial to architectural design, the quality of the motivation and the character of the significance being revealed by the architecture. This is another way of saying that a society is reflected in its architecture. Spiritual architecture reflects the spiritual condition of the people who build. But it is an error to suppose that great buildings are directly proportional to spiritual health. Spiritual architecture is concerned with the aspirations of individuals and groups.

*Monumental architecture* is, by definition, committed to remembrance and so to the appearance of permanence. The simple repose of massive earth-borne structures and trilithonic openings are preferred to enigmatic balances and controlled thrusts. Symmetry of plan goes with the stable symmetry of structure. Monumental architecture is concerned primarily with the dead and may anticipate in life the honours to be paid to the departed.

*Utilitarian architecture* is, by definition, dedicated to utility, and the expression of function becomes architectural homage to a non-spiritual objective. Utilitarian architecture is materialistic. Materialism can recognise no values outside itself and the utilitarian building is self-justifying in terms of its utility. Utilitarian architecture is the reflection of material achievement seen as an end in itself.

*The useful therefore beautiful argument implies a non-material value—beauty—but it is also invalid on other grounds.*

*See Appendix*

*This is not intended to be a pejorative statement.*

The five kinds of architecture can and do co-exist. There are indications that none of them completely nor all of them together can entirely satisfy our modern needs though all of them have specific relevance to specific human problems and physical situations.

All architecture conditions the environment in which people live and have their being. Our lives are partly automatic, partly chance-directed, partly conditioned by society, partly acted according to parts we create for ourselves. We play our parts in scenery which is mainly architectural. What we call the environment is our stage and its character affects the parts which it is possible for us to play.

*cf. Scenic architecture; p.74*

Architecture is not only an expression of what men are: it reflects back upon men and conditions what it is possible for them to be and to become.

Man's relationship with his environment is a two-way traffic. Abuse begets degeneration. Harmony fosters peace.

The five kinds of architecture were cut off at the roots by the 'modern movement' which substituted a single formula which was artificial, mechanistic, functional, inhuman, totalitarian. Yet by its concentration upon function and rationality in the use of new materials, during the early stages of the movement it greatly enlarged the possibilities of comfort and convenience.

The plants cut off at the roots, the five basic kinds of architecture, have grown up again in a straggling fashion through the prisms of modernism.

It would be a sad mistake to reject what was achieved by the 'modern movement'. What we must now seek is a way of cultivating architecture like a garden of different kinds of plants, not like a potato field. We are seeking a *humane architecture*. Analogously we may call this a concept of the garden not of the single crop.

*The 'modern movement' contributed to enlightenment but it would be naive, or extremely pessimistic, to think that it was the end of the road.*

## 2. ETHICAL CONFUSION

By identifying different kinds of architecture we may avoid judging one kind by standards appropriate only to another, but if a theory of architecture is to perform its dual role of helping us to make judgments in the process of design and providing criteria for assessment of the finished product, we must avoid a confusion of aesthetics with ethics. It is necessary to say this because utilitarianism and utilitarian architecture are prone to become confused with morality.

Folk and vernacular architecture being traditional and customary require good manners rather than morality. Spiritual architecture, of its own nature, may be seen to transcend human morals. Monumental architecture, in being concerned with honour and pride, is open to moral judgment, but this relates to the programme rather than to the design. In utilitarian architecture, based upon fitness for purpose, the ethicality of the purpose may be questioned, in like manner to the appropriateness of a monument, but this is external to design. The degree of fitness, however, and the notion of conceiving a perfect solution encourage us, indeed compel us to make judgments between better and worse, good and bad. But in using the words good or bad we are not making a moral judgment: we have moved out of the broadly classified field of human thinking which is defined as *ethics* into *aesthetics* where the word good refers to quality.

The distinction between good and poor quality is clear to most people. There is good cloth and less-good cloth. It is not immoral to make an expensive coat out of good cloth or a cheap coat out of relatively poor cloth. A coat is an artifact; so is a building, and the distinction between good and bad is a

*It is obviously absurd to judge Gothic architecture by the standards of Sianan or Palladio and it is important to recognise that value judgments imply the existence of a basis from which such judgments are to be made. For renaissance theorists this basis was absolute: since c. 1745 it has been relative or subjective.*

*Value judgments are still relative to a system of belief even when this is reduced to the artist's belief in himself.*

*Our present need is to try to understand the nature of architecture. This is the general attitude of science—to seek understanding rather than to judge.*

distinction of quality. This presents quite enough problems without introducing any moral problems proper to the study of ethics. It is sufficient for our present purpose to state a moral belief that architecture should be good—it is good that architecture should be good. The first good is an ethical good, the second is aesthetic. Our problem is to discover an acceptable basis for qualitative assessments in the making of architecture.

In order to do this we must exclude consideration of the ethicality of the programme, not, it must be emphasised, because the ethicality of the programme is unimportant, but because it is irrelevant to our present task. To many people this may seem to be an outrageous statement and the matter might be argued at great length. It could be said, quite truly, that the social value of a building, of a school as compared with a casino, for example, is an important consideration. It is; but it is not an architectural consideration.

It may be agreed that the Church of Santa Sophia which was built for Justinian in Constantinople was and still is a great work of architecture. Its change of use to being a mosque did not alter this, and now it is a museum. Most medieval castles are totally obsolete but they have not ceased to be architecture. The same could be said of palaces and temples and the ruined Bridge of Avignon. The great palaces of St Petersburg are still the treasures of Leningrad. Much fine architecture has been built by people of questionable virtue for purposes which we may disapprove.

The moral standards and practices of any society have an effect upon architecture, upon what it is possible to build. Priority may be given to interest rates over social need as, for example, when offices and shops take precedence over houses and factories or vice versa. A moral disapproval of office blocks or shopping centres in a given social context does not inhibit the design of good rather than bad architecture.

As a citizen an architect may (perhaps should, but that is a matter for his own conscience), refuse to be involved in an activity of which he morally disapproves, but this ethical problem must lie outside the scope of our present enquiry into the theory of architecture as such.

A book on the ethics of architecture would be about the architect's responsibilities in practice: responsibilities to society and to his fellow architects. To design well is one of those responsibilities. This book is about designing well and must take account of the requirements of people in so far as they affect design. Social responsibility is implicit in all that follows but in order to avoid utter confusion we must draw as clear a line as possible between ethical and aesthetic considerations.

*It is interesting that 'bad' architecture has often been well-built out of expensive materials. It has been the better for this. The contrary is also apparent. Good design has been marred by poor materials and workmanship. Proportion is relevant. See p.61*

# 3. AESTHETICS

By derivation aesthetics is concerned with feeling and by custom with beauty. The human activity which links emotion with the creation and appreciation of beautiful things is called art, and many philosophers have simplified the problems of aesthetics by assuming that the objective of art is the creation of beautiful artifacts. Even so the definition of beauty has presented insuperable difficulties. But from the earliest times it has been apparent that, in the practice of activities which we call artistic, it has been possible to produce works that express feelings which by no reasonable stretch of meaning can possibly be called beautiful, emotions of horror, hate, disgust, fear, cruelty, pride and so on, as well as emotions which art can interpret but for which we have no names. Just as renaissance astronomers used every device which they could conceive to reconcile observed aberrations with the dogma that the orbits of planets were circular, so philosophers and critics have endeavoured to maintain that even the most abominable subjects and loathsome feelings are transmuted into beauty by the process of art.

Few people now persist in believing that the earth has a circular orbit: rather more continue to think that art is a way of transmuting base feelings and hideous events into pure beauty. A more acceptable view would be that the artist is a man who has the skill to interpret and convey, through an artistic medium, emotion generated in a hyper-sensitive person by an acute awareness of phenomena. He is an interpreter, a revealer and a creator of, among other things, beauty, but beauty is manifestly not the objective of much that we customarily recognise as being art.

*An indication of the nature of art.*

In architectural aesthetics, however, it has often been assumed that the aim of the architect is to produce beautiful buildings, that the standard of criticism should be a beauty standard. Renaissance architecture was founded, mainly by Alberti, upon the belief that beauty is a quality of things which are in themselves and apart from all circumstance and opinion, of their own nature, beautiful. He believed that the ancients, the architects of Greek and Roman times, had discovered the secrets of making things beautiful. He proceeded, with a scientific integrity almost unique in his time, to probe behind the ancient architecture which exemplified beauty, in order to discover its underlying principles and produce a theoretical basis for the practical design of modern architecture. By the middle of the sixteenth century the scientific basis had been forgotten and rules were codified by such architects as Palladio. The philosophic principle that beauty was the aim, and could be achieved by conformity to

*Classicism is based upon an objective view of beauty.*

law, was a basic assumption for all who practised classical design. In Philibert de l'Orme's book *L'Architecture* the renaissance aesthetic came into headlong collision with a rationality derived from the medieval tradition of the master masons and the traditions of folk architecture; but the main current of European, and latterly American, practice was classical and conformed to the assumption that beauty was inherent; a fact not a matter of opinion.

Classical aesthetics had the advantage of avoiding the hedonistic definition of beauty which, apart from its other disadvantages, was uncongenial to the upper levels of a stratified society. Beauty was the predictable result of the application of scientific laws. Unfortunately the science upon which the laws were founded proved, by the middle of the seventeenth century, to be almost completely untrue. The *method* of Alberti was sound but the data available to him were not; and nobody attempted to up-date the theory of architecture in the light of new scientific knowledge.

The practical advantage of the classical system of design was that it justified a way of designing architecture which had evolved slowly and had been worked upon by many minds over a long period. It was the result of matured artistic experience and can be seen as the folk architecture of a social élite. It came to mean, for the gentry and the clergy of the western world, what folk architecture meant to the peasants, yeomen and burghers. It was subtly modified to the taste of emerging nations, so producing recognisable differentiations, without any deep differences of aesthetic principle, in societies with a common culture and the seeds of disastrous dispute.

There are people who see the practical advantages of adhering to the classical aesthetic, but nowadays the only argument can be reduced to the plea that expediency justifies the covering up of false foundations. The theoretical basis of classical aesthetics is no longer acceptable as true.

Though the first major theoretical attack upon the practice of classicism came from Philibert de l'Orme in 1567 it was not until the mid-eighteenth century that the philosophical foundations were demolished. This happened in England and is most clearly seen in David Hume's essay *On the Standard of Taste*. Beauty is not objective: it is not inherent in objects, it is a matter of opinion. But whose opinion? To the English gentry of the eighteenth century it was a matter of *Taste* which was formed by the concurrence of cultivated minds and sensitivities. By the end of the next century we find a great artist, Leo Tolstoy, asserting that it was to be revealed by the judgment of simple peasants.

In modern times the philosophical consideration of art has shifted from beauty to emotion and although art has in

*De l'Orme came of a family of master masons. In the context of the Renaissance he was a rebel but not a reactionary. He was far ahead of his time in ideas about the relationship of architecture to people.*

*Hedonism links beauty with enjoyment. What we like is therefore beautiful— whoever we may be! Subjectively there must be an element of truth in this.*

*The importance of accumulated experience in classical architecture should not be neglected. It is still relevant simply because it does embody so much from the work of generations of talented creative designers. The aesthetic is corrupt but the experience is real and the artifacts have achieved great beauty.*

*See Tolstoy, What is Art? (London 1898). The first edition in Russian, 1897, was censored and Tolstoy preferred the English translation.*
*'A good and lofty work of art may be incomprehensible, but not to simple, unperverted peasant labourers...... it may be, and often is, unintelligible to erudite, perverted people destitute of religion.' (translation by Aylmer Maude).*

fact taken over, to a considerable extent, the role of philosophy in exploring the nature of things, it is commonly seen as being a way of expressing emotions and the vulgar opinion is that art *is* self-expression. Architecture has not been unaffected by this expressionistic aesthetic, but the serious artist in any medium knows by experience that little if anything can be done under the actual stress of deep emotion and that most works of art, as much the architecture of the concert hall as the music of the symphony, require sustained work over a long period. Little if any great art is the direct and immediate expression of the artist's own emotion. A lyric could be but an epic, no. Furthermore many works of art are not individual productions. The composer cannot complete his symphony by performing it himself. The architect is a member of a complex team. The successful practice of any art is a much more serious discipline than most people realise.

If we try to consider architecture in terms of the expression of emotion we must distinguish between the possible expression of the artist's own emotions about anything or everything, which it would seem to be impossible to express in, for example, the building of a warehouse for animal feeding stuffs, and his feeling for the functional and structural problems inherent in the problem of designing such a warehouse. The former is absurd, the latter is highly relevant. Art proceeds where reason cannot follow. Important though rationality is, art employs the mind at levels of feeling and intuition which have proved more important than reasoning in the development of the human species.

*Art does, however, contain its own logic and discipline. This is different from what we think of as reasoning. It is in another dimension of the mind.*

If we are to believe that there is some common ground in all the different arts, and if we accept the intuition of our age that art is related to the emotions of people, rather than to an ideal concept of beauty, the relevance of emotion to architecture cannot be self-expression and must reside in the emotional relationship between the architect's cognition of the subject-matter of the architecture (the programme) and his para-intellectual synthesis of his own understanding of the problem and its solution in architectural terms.

This points to something much more useful than a definition of architecture: it indicates the special qualities of mind and personality which makes a person capable of producing architecture, that is, of being an architect. He or she must have a developed talent for understanding a human complex of needs and interpreting them through feeling, intuition and reasoning in terms of built form within an environmental context.

*The nature of an architect.*

A *developed talent* implies, in the first place a talent and in the second a process of cultivation through exercises and disciplines. *Understanding* implies feeling-with, that · is sympathy (the opposite of which is arrogance). *Interpretation through feeling* implies the suppression of individuality and the exposure of one's own emotions to the problems of other people. (This is not easy but is consonant with the experience of all artists.) *Intuition* is something we do not understand, but in the present context it is the power of creating, of creating what has never before existed in relation to the needs which have been apprehended. Reasoning is only valid when it follows feeling and intuition which provide essential data but there is already a lot of data in the programme and the preliminary inspection of it which must be fed back. Separation for the purposes of consideration in words, which must of necessity be in an intelligible sequence, tends to mask the fact that the human brain is capable of feeling, intuiting, examining and reasoning all at the same time. We cultivate ourselves in separate ways but we use our cultivated talents and techniques simultaneously like the instruments in an orchestra.

In the early twentieth century there was a reaction against the expression of specific emotions in art; against subject-matter in pictures and styles in architecture. Much of this was crypto-classical and proceeded through Clive Bell's concept of 'significant form' to culmination in Le Corbusier's *Le Modulor*. But abstract art was more than an attempt to re-establish classicism. It recognised in the West what had long been known in the East, and especially to artists who worked under the religious prohibition of Islam, that shapes and arrangements and even natural objects such as weathered roots of trees, can have meaning without having specific meaning. This was obvious to primitive peoples who decorated with what we call geometrical patterns. Even the discovery by Art Nouveau artists that non-geometrical pattern could have emotional connotations was not new at all. It was very primitive and basic and goes back beyond the ability of man to represent anything by a specific image; a man by a picture of a man, for example. It goes back to the awareness of the significance of a shape, to the fear and veneration of an evocative symbol. Such art represents nothing but is something.

*Meaning without specificity. Art can 'say' things that can only be apprehended in that way.*

*Art as essence.*

A distinction is often made between representational and non-representational art. This is a misunderstanding. No art merely represents, it interprets. Even a camera in its blundering, unfeeling, technology-conditioned way, interprets if you point it at anything and press the trigger. Photography as an art, which it certainly is, depends upon the interpretation of the subject which a photographer wishes to make and feels to be relevant and decides to achieve.

Abstract art is not meaningless but its meaning is irrelevant to anything outside itself. It is an essence, in the proper sense of that word, an 'isness'.

Abstract art, as practised by such masters as Mondrian and Nicholson, seemed to provide a clue to designing modern architecture, and many buildings in the mid-twentieth century echoed the forms and arrangements of abstract art as well as employing abstract painting and sculptures as a form of decoration. But architecture is not abstract: it is always relative to people—dead or alive. It always has specific meaning and relevance to people so, if we look at it honestly, abstractation in architecture was a, kind of pastiche, a simulation, a borrowing of forms which were independent of humanity.

The experimentalism of abstract art degenerated to become the stock-in-trade of the basic art courses in colleges. The reiteration of this 'kid's stuff' on the elevations of buildings which purport .to be serious works of art was pathetic. We have moved on from that. Architecture cannot be independent of function, or of people, neither of which are abstract. For a time the clichés of abstract painting and sculpture provided a decorative system for architecture, a decorative system which was thought to involve the whole three-dimensional building, but it was really only a stylistic borrowing and never a true part of architecture. It did not, however, inhibit the possibility of designing great architecture any more than the Gothic Revival did. It was a superficiality.

Symbolism, however, has to be distinguished from abstraction. Strictly speaking a symbol cannot be abstract. It is a symbol of something yet, as has been indicated above, a non-representational shape can have meaning, attract veneration and become a veritable symbol. This can happen to architecture as, for example, the tower of the Palace of Westminster with its clock, Big Ben.

It is possible to design symbols, indeed they have become endemic in the publicity business, but symbolism is always a relationship not an independent inherent condition of an object. Big Ben does not mean to a Frenchman what it does to an Englishman. A thistle is a weed except to the Scots. The evocative properties of shapes are a mystery which psychology has hardly begun to recognise, let alone explain, while artists continue to explore; but symbolism, for practical purposes, is a relationship between an object and people. Usually it is specific though sometimes, especially in religion, it is mysterious and mystery is cultivated, de-mystification being opposed and resented. To confuse a symbol with what it symbolises is superstitious. Just as 'beauty' does not reside in the object so *power* does not reside in the symbol. Architects may often

*Symbolism is never abstract.*

make use of symbolism and most monumental architecture is symbolic, but it cannot be the basis of an aesthetic.

It is atavistic for modern man to attempt to recover an absolute system of aesthetic values but this does not necessarily imply that the alternative is a wayward empiricism in which every designer pleases himself and there are no standards, any more than the inconceivability of a beginning or an end to time inhibits the use of clocks.

The great renaissance theorist, Alberti, was not a fool: he was a genius who saw, far ahead of his time, that theory must proceed by careful assembly of evidence and examination of the facts in a way which we now call scientific. Nearly all Alberti's supposed facts turned out later to be wrong but his method was valid. Architecture is a phenomenon which can be investigated and it has the advantage that it has existed for thousands of years and examples are distributed over the surface of the Earth. Few fields of scientific research have such a wealth of evidence over such a long time-span.

An important function of architectural history is to examine this evidence and set it in its correct social context so that the evidence of buildings can be related to the people by whom and for whom the architecture was made; thus the history of architecture becomes a study of the relationship of people to architecture over a long time-span and a basis for thinking about the problems of modern architecture, but it also helps us to place the right interpretation upon the built evidence in looking for constants and variables in architectural design and trying to deduce the architectural facts of life. As in the evolution of biological species so in architecture, failure tends to be discarded. Are there any constant factors of success?

Alberti also turned to the most advanced physical sciences of his day and enquired how their laws impinged upon architecture. We can do the same in our time and surprisingly little attempt has been made to do so in the light of modern scientific thinking since Alberti. His cosmology for example, was completely wrong; ours is certainly imperfect but modern knowledge ought to yield better and more accurate results than could be obtained in the fifteenth century.

In the next section we shall look first at physical laws and theories which directly affect the phenomenon of architecture and then at the ways in which architects have come to terms with these laws and the necessities of building.

*The relevance of History to practice. History is only one moment behind the present and everything we do is in process of taking place in history. History is the continuum: we are creating incidents.*

## 4. THE PHYSICAL EVIDENCE

Science rests upon one fundamental assumption which so far has proved to be correct. It is that the world is rational and consistent, that an experiment repeated under identical conditions will produce the same result; that one law derived from hypothesis and experimental confirmation will not contradict another and likewise that extrapolations, mainly by mathematical methods, beyond the range of observable evidence will all fit into a single consistent whole.

*This chapter concentrates upon one aspect as a stage in making a mosaic of understanding. We are isolating the physical facts in order to relate them to a whole which is not yet apparent.*

The stupendous fact is that all the evidence accumulated by science indicates a rational world, and not only rational but perceptible as rational by human beings. In other words it conforms to *our* concept of rationality. It is true that much remains mysterious, and science has so far refrained from investigation of some areas of experience, but the faith of our time is that the world, the whole cosmos and not just our planet, our system, our galaxy, is designed in an orderly rational way. This was also believed by the Greeks of ancient times and by Alberti. It was, and perhaps still is, a reasonable assumption that architecture should conform to the order of the universe, not contradict it. The model for design in architecture was the design of the universe and if we believe that design cannot exist without a designer we must attribute, as Alberti did, divine sanction to architecture which conforms to the laws of nature. God stood for order and harmony, disorder and unrest were the antithesis of God. Even if this is not true it has to be taken into account simply because so many people have believed and still do believe it to be true. Since complete knowledge is inconceivable and unattainable, what is believed at any time in history is more effective than what may be true. The great achievements of renaissance architects were based upon belief, not truth. But belief was founded upon truth so far as it was known. We can believe in truth but we cannot found anything substantial upon what we know to be untrue. In our time we can only found our architectural theory upon what we understand of the truth It is unthinkable that we should found it upon what we know to be false.

*One cannot refrain from the word 'designed' despite the implications which lie outside the scope of this book.*

If we consider the phenomenon of architecture as being, like the phenomenon of man, a part of nature, it is reasonable to expect it to harmonise with not contradict the laws of nature, but it is necessary to reiterate that this is not a moral matter. If we say that a stone thrown into a pond *should* sink we are not making a moral judgment, we are expecting it to conform with the law of gravity; nor are we yet making an aesthetic judgment.

*It follows that classical theory, despite all its beneficial results, cannot be accepted as being true.*

*The term 'The Phenomenon of Man' is the title of one of the seminal books of the twentieth century, by Teilhard de Chardin. (English edition, London 1959). Ideas from this book permeate the present work and are further discussed in my book* Civilization—the Next Stage *(Newcastle 1969 and Tokyo 1977).*

All buildings have mass and rest upon the ground. This is a fact no matter what devices architects may use to disguise it. A slab building supported on *pilotti* or a pair of Byzantine stilted arches supported centrally on a narrow column, emphasise mass and diminish support visually. At first sight this may appear to be a falsification, but look at a tree or a bullrush or most flowering plants. Slender stems support apparently massive superstructures. By comparison with building techniques a humble daisy in flower is a marvellously refined and sophisticated structure. We may observe that simple structures which obviously rest firmly on the earth convey an impression of repose, but what a lot of pleasure we should be denying ourselves were we to insist, as classical architects tended to do, that this appearance of repose and stability was obligatory. It is, however, useful as a design aid, to observe that an obviously stable structure has qualities which are natural to it and apprehended by people who do not think about structural principles. Likewise the airy counterpoise of a Gothic cathedral belongs to an architecture which can be understood at sophisticated levels of structural awareness but is appreciated emotionally by people who have no such knowledge.

cf. Tolstoy, p.13

Gravity and all the related forces in a structure need to be understood by the designer so that he knows what he is doing. It is not simply a question of stability—safety factors can ensure that but the result is cautious, perhaps brutal.

What we are seeking is a refinement of structure for which standards are set in nature.

Balance as we see it in a simple pair of scales or a see-saw is obviously related to terrestrial gravity. Equal weights at equal distances from the fulcrum will balance, and this is important in architecture both structurally and visually. We seem to extrapolate from the idea of a physical balance to a visual one and an obvious imbalance has the property of looking unbalanced: lop-sided, as we say opprobriously.

Most things which move directionally are symmetrical about the axis of movement. This is true about flies and aeroplanes, ships and human beings, but the symmetrical appearance does not reflect entirely symmetrical internal arrangements. In man, for example, the heart is on one side and the liver on the other but an imbalance of eyes or ears is considered unpleasant. Classical theorists rightly saw a connection between human ideas of visual propriety and the form of the human body. Symmetry is a form of balance which is easy to apprehend though it involves subtlety and judgment in design, the achievement of a different kind of balance in adjusting internal functions to external appearance. The problem is simply posed in the design of a bus where the overall appearance is symmetrical on the directional axis, the passengers are symmetrically seated but the driver sits to one side. The headlamps are symmetrical but the steering wheel is not.

Frontal symmetry in the human figure is complemented by asymmetry in profile. Seen from the side the human figure is directional and capable of balancing in a vertical position or in movement when the balance is complex, variable and includes a component of movement.

But buildings do not move. Is it sensible to compare them with aeroplanes, buses or men? Certainly the fact that buildings are static removes some of the reasons for symmetry. There is no dynamic component in the building itself. It is static but we are not. Our relationship is the same as to a statue. To inspect it we move round it. Alternatively we put it on a turn-table. Either we move or it moves. With a building it has to be us and our visual knowledge of the building is formed by a series of impressions during which the parts of the building move in relation to each other (parallax) as seen by us.

In movement we may become aware of imbalance, of ungainliness, as with an obese human figure seen in profile. Our sense of visual decorum which derives from awareness of our own human form is not irrelevant to our appreciation of static objects. Nor is balance such a simple matter as it first appears to be. There is a time component for all conceivable shapes except perfect spheres. The sphere is the same from all points of view, around, above and below. It is modified by perspective, consistently in relation to distance whatever the direction of observation, but we apprehend it as a sphere and this fact of total consistency has interested philosophers and artists for a very long time. But even the sphere is modified visually by light and shade. It is not accidental that the dome has commonly been thought of as the strongest architectural form.

In plan, section and elevation the sphere is a circle and architects have been interested in its completeness and unity. If the acme of design is, as Alberti and many others have thought it to be, the achievement of a unity to which nothing could be added and from which nothing could be subtracted without disadvantage, or as Alberti (translated by Leoni) put it, 'making it homely and disagreeable', then the circle is the standard of perfection. Its mathematical properties are fascinating and it can contain or be contained by all the regular geometrical figures from the equilateral triangle to infinity. It was mainly because of this evident perfection that astronomers and theologians alike strove, as mentioned above, to maintain the concept of circular planetary orbits, thus

*The most obvious demonstration of parallax is to hold one's hands up, fingers apart, one hand behind the other and move one hand, or move one's head. There is relative displacement. This is of fundamental importance to designers (see Thomas, B. Geometry in Pictorial Composition, Newcastle 1971).*

ignoring the effect of motion upon the true and more complex balance which is achieved by the elliptical orbits.

But the circle is more than a fascinating geometrical figure. It is also the mandala, the symbol of the amazing intuition of eastern philosphers that balance is fundamental to the nature of things, to the very existence of the universe. This is an intuition which science increasingly tends to confirm whether we look at the stars, at atomic physics or at ecology. Psychology begins to confirm the validity of eastern techniques of cultivating balance in the human personality.

Throughout nature there are balances. It appears that even matter may have a counterpart in anti-matter, and all being consists in an infinitude of interactions. Balance is in the nature of things and every imbalance tends towards a new balance.

People have a sense of balance, not only physically, as in walking a tight-rope, but mentally and emotionally. This is relevant to the way architects design buildings and the way in which they are experienced by people.

Proportion is related to balance and gravity. Our sense of proportion is partly synonymous with sense of balance but also relates to our feeling for appropriate imbalance. Complete calm may be an objective but the way is out of activity and all building is the product of activity, not contemplation (though that has a part in the process of design). Where equilibrium does not exist there is movement and the question is how much is acceptable. The answer would seem to be, only so much as is compatible with a new balance. For example acceleration is a good quality in a vehicle but if it tears the tyres off it is out of proportion. We must adjust the acceleration or improve the tyres. Thus the sense of proportion is partly based upon awareness of what is practical.

But practicality is not only physical. A funeral procession for a Soviet minister led by drum-majorettes and a silver band playing *Yankee Doodle* is not physically impossible or even difficult to arrange but it is inappropriate, in bad taste, out of proportion. There is a famous film, *Tunes of Glory*, in which the macabre and tragic climax is the ordering of a Field Marshal's funeral for a lieutenant-colonel by a major with a guilty and deranged mind. Admittedly all feelings of appropriateness are conditioned by the standards, the conventions of the society in which people live, but this is a fact of life: people *do* live in communities which *do* have conventions. 'Manners Maketh Man' is a motto which enshrines a truth, namely, that men cannot live in communities without agreed and accepted rules of behaviour. This is basic to animal behaviour quite apart from civilised human communities.

*A useful introduction to this concept is* Mandala *by José and Miriam Argüelles (Berkeley & London 1972).*

**Chinese Yang-Yin symbol**

*Played by John Mills and Alec Guiness respectively.*

*Motto of William of Wykeham 1324-1404.*

But for architects proportion has for ages meant the relationship between the parts of a building and renaissance theory attempted to relate proportion to physical laws deduced mainly from corrupt evidence. Yet the acceptance of certain proportions and the rejection of all others had beneficial results. It imposed upon architecture a consistency within each building and between one building and another which established easily recognisable relationships.

The sense of proportion is not entirely subjective. It can be rationalised to explain why some proportions are more pleasing than others and these rationalisations need not now be based upon the false evidence and analogies used by Alberti.

*There is plenty of scope for modern research into proportion in architecture.*

*See Prak, op.cit.*

The words horizontal and vertical are ways of specifying what is at right angles to the surface of the earth and what is parallel to a tangent to its circumference. Every shape in architecture can be assessed in terms of horizontality and verticality. But the square, the circle and the polygons with even numbers of sides are neutral; equally horizontal and vertical. Slopes of 45° are neutral. Less than 45° tends to the horizontal and more tends to the vertical. We speak of a building as having horizontality or verticality and a whole range of impressions and associations relate to verticality and horizontality. Classical theory, with its intuition for balance and its rationalisation which took the form of valuing the mean between extremes, advocated rooms which were cubic or multiples of cubes. The square end wall gave emphasis neither to height nor width. But the most important problems of proportion arose with openings in walls and spaces between columns. Alberti related the two and saw all building as if it were columnar whether the columns were expressed or not. This he called 'compartition'. Each compartment had a proportion of width to height, and so did windows within the compartments. The eighteenth-century French theorist Laugier went so far as to regard the openings, the windows in walls, as architectural blemishes which, being practical necessities in many buildings, he admitted as '*licenses*'.

In contrast to interior design, square compartition was eschewed because it did not reflect the traditional spacing of columns which conformed to the practicalities of spanning between them with stone lintels. Although renaissance buildings were not framed structures (apart from open colonnades), Alberti actually anticipated the structural frame in his aesthetic theory of compartition and the term is more relevant to modern buildings than to renaissance palaces in Italy. When we express the structural frame in the facade we create compartments and the proportions of these com-

**Compartition. The Palazzo Rucellai in Florence by Alberti.**

*This is an interesting example of the eye becoming accustomed to the usual way of building. Taste has roots in custom.*

partments. the proportions of any windows in them and the relation of compartition to the shape and proportions of the whole building are current problems of design.

Taking a clue from music, renaissance theorists believed that the relationship of the dimensions of pipes and tubes to the musical consonances or dissonances they produce could be transferred to architecture. Knowing nothing of sound waves they thought that visual harmony and musical harmony must be reflections of the harmony of the world. The harmony does exist but sight and sound operate on different wavelengths.

Classical theory accepted ratios based upon acoustics as being valid for the visual arts and the prescribed proportions for openings were whole-number ratios—1 : 2, 1 : 3 being, for practical reasons, the most common, but they also accepted the golden mean (a line so divided that the ratio of its smaller part to its larger part is the same as the ratio of its larger part to the whole length) and the ratio of the side of a square to its diagonal, 1 : $\sqrt{2}$ on the authority of the ancients. 1 : $\sqrt{2}$ is said by Alberti, with characteristic honesty, to be a mystery, but in fact the acceptance of the first irrational number as valid in proportional theory was its condemnation. None the less, the consistency of proportion which resulted from limiting the acceptable possibilities to, in effect, four, gave a consistency to design which was peaceful. All architecturally acceptable openings had verticality in classical architecture but mannerists deliberately used squares and horizontal openings to defy propriety ('for kicks' as it were).

The foundations of renaissance proportional theory have been undermined, but did they reach a valid conclusion by the wrong route? We are not wrong in admiring a Palladian building. It has stood the test of time and changing fashion. But if the theory upon which it was designed is wrongly founded how comes it about that we still think it is an admirable building?

The answer to this lies not in the details of the system of proportion which Alberti bequeathed to Palladio: it is to be found in the overall concept of harmony of all the parts within a whole that was a resultant unity. Other proportions and dimensions could have achieved this but only when the intention was to create the calm repose of a unified design (*cf.* mandalas) in which all the parts are consistent with the whole. The ratio of width to height being 1 : 3 is no more valid than it being 1 : 2·85 though there is a subtle difference comparable with the musical difference between the key of C major and C#major. What matters is, to continue the musical allusion, that it is all in the same key. The design is consistent: the proportion runs right through.

*See Wittkower, R.* Architectural Principles in the Age of Humanism *(London 1952) and Allsopp, B.* A History of Renaissance Architecture *(London 1959) Chapter III.*

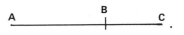

**Golden Section. BC : AB :: AB : AC**

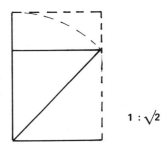

**1 : $\sqrt{2}$**

**Calm** *is a quality of most good architecture.*

There is another basis for proportion. This can be demonstrated by such a creature as the crane fly—the 'daddy long-legs'. Structurally his legs are amazing. In proportion to his body they are as long as they can possibly be. Now if we were to double the size of his body those legs would be too thin to support his weight and they would have to be thicker, and at some stage in the enlargement of this fly we should reach a point at which the weight of the legs would be such that he could no longer fly at all and he would be more like a spider. This phenomenon is well known to all who make models and is called 'scale effect'. There is a natural limit to the size of anything beyond which it is no longer viable as what it is and can only survive, if at all, by becoming something else. This is a matter of proportion and is highly relevant to architecture. There are structural limits to size but more importantly there are functional limits. Educational administrators may decide to build a school with so many pupils that it is impossible to design it. A hospital conceived on standards of administrative and clinical convenience alone may be such that it is impossible to design it satisfactorily as a building. The study of proportion implies the determination of the right size for a building and this is not just a matter of opinion any more than the impossibility of doubling of the size of the crane fly is.

*Natural proportion.*

*RIGHT SIZE*

We have already noticed that structural properties affect proportion but this control is no longer relevant because structural devices for increasing the real strength of beams (such as pre-stressing) have made visual assessment of suitability impossible. If truthful expression were a criterion of architecture this would be the area of greatest dishonesty. When it is necessary to have a specification and a computer to assess the structural validity of a span, any basis for understanding of proportion based upon structure has vanished. In effect the structural limits of horizontality have been stretched to a point far beyond aesthetic necessity.

*Structural proportion.*

Finally there is the relationship of structure to man. This is perhaps the most important aspect of proportion and leads us to consideration of scale. All buildings relate to the size of the people who will use them. In twelfth-century castles, essentially utilitarian military buildings, the size of doors tell us that the people were generally small by our standards. This is attested by effigies and skeletons. The proportions of a man, his overall width to his height, indicate the natural proportions of a doorway, proportions to which we have become accustomed through generations of usage. But we do not always want minimum sizes and the way of scaling-up in proportion is familiar. We maintain the same proportion by projecting the diagonal to increase the size.

*SCALE*

Proportion related to the human form has long been recognised as a basic module of architecture and consistency of proportion is recognised as a humane and peaceful characteristic in design. Extrapolations from abstract painting and sculpture in modern times have vitiated this innate human relationship. As we have noticed above, the canons of abstract art are misleading for architecture which is a social art in that it must always relate to man.

*Generally good scale in a building means a consistent relationship to the human figure throughout the design, but relationship to the environment is also important and in moving from outside to inside a subtle transition of scale has to be made. A 'great' architect reveals his quality in his handling of architectural scale.*

## 5. THE EMOTIONAL EVIDENCE

In the study of aesthetics attention has been directed mainly to emotion expressed and emotion aroused. Of the latter Collingwood said that it was corrupt for an artist to seek to arouse specific or calculated emotions in his audience: this was not art but propaganda, advertising, persuasion or magic. Undoubtedly works of art can and do arouse emotion but the emotion varies from person to person. The work of art may express emotion but there is no way of telling that the emotion expressed will be the emotion aroused. For example the poet may write, 'I do intend in very part to live and die for thee' and some reader may comment 'Poor sap!' That architects can and do set out to arouse emotion in buildings which are pretentious is ubiquitously obvious, particularly in commercial buildings which become advertising material rather than architecture. This is widely believed by artists to be not-art.

It is even more widely believed by artists and people in general that art can express feeling and that this is a primary purpose of art. The response of the audience is not conditioned by the artist; it depends upon appreciation, an ability to receive what is expressed. Criticism and teaching are often directed towards helping people to receive what might otherwise be inaccessible to them. It has already been said that architecture is an improper medium for the expression of kinds of emotion which might be expressed quite properly in poetry, painting or music. This is not the place to discuss the role of artists in society, important, indeed vital, though this may be. We are only concerned with architects. Almost always they are commissioned by people to design buildings which the architect himself will neither pay for nor inhabit, and may seldom or never see, but they create the environment, set the stage, for other people's lives. The architect, like any good workman, may, and one may think should, take a justified pride in doing his job well but this excludes almost,

*In recent times.*

*Collingwood, R.G.* The Principles of Art *(Oxford 1938).*

if not quite entirely, the expression of idiosyncratic feelings of the man apart from his role as architect. A feeling of elation because it is a beautiful spring morning does not justify an efflorescence of pinnacles on a design for a police station.

The feelings which are proper to be expressed in architecture are of two kinds. The first kind is feelings for the actual stuff of architecture, materials, structure, texture, colour, function, space, proportion etc. The second kind is feelings for and sympathy with the people who will use and behold and live with the building, together with feelings for the relationship with its environment. Ability to feel for and with and through these two groups of things must be the basis of architectural education, the cultivation in the medium of architecture of some degree of talent for creative design.

But aesthetics, and indeed the profession of architecture, have taken little notice of another sort of feeling which is of crucial importance. This is a feeling for the feelings of other people about everything to do with our environment.

Such feelings are mainly traditional and derive from what people are accustomed to. It has to be recognised that people have a sense of place and like the comfort of the familiar. The *genius loci* is not just a fancied pagan spirit but a sensitivity in people for the characteristics of locality. Where folk architecture survives the spirit of the place is easy to diagnose, but in soiled industrialised environments the manifestations of the genius may be pathetically meagre, yet, on that account, all the more precious to people.

Change is not good in itself any more than architecture is beautiful by some absolute standard. Change affects people and can destroy their sense of place. Too much change creates neuroses in the individual and in society. The means of assimilating, of adjusting healthily to change in environment, is the preservation of *significant appearance*.

This has been fundamental to architectural design from the earliest times. When changes in structure, material and technique occur, the social-emotional adjustment is made, and always has been made, by preserving the old appearance in the new technique and letting the visual transition take place gradually, often over several generations. The most famous example of the principle of preserving significant appearance is in the evolution of the Greek Doric order from timber to stone. The timber forms, slightly modified by two centuries of experience, are embodied in the Parthenon which has commonly been regarded as the most nearly perfect building in the world. A more modern example is the use of fabric or wood-grain appearances on plastics—an extension by modern technology of the eighteenth-century technique of veneering.

*This is a condensation of ideas which I have developed in other books especially* Art and the Nature of Architecture *(London 1952) and* Towards a Humane Architecture *(London 1974).*

*SIGNIFICANT APPEARANCE*

The architectural puritan may condemn this as immoral, untruthful expression; but the question is whether it is more important to express melamine-formaldehyde plastics as dull brown sheets than it is to relate design to the comfort, convenience and pleasure of people. Throughout architectural history appearance has followed custom and the evolution of the multitudinous styles of architecture has been profoundly affected by the continuing human desire to preserve appearances and come to terms with novelties slowly. Evidence accumulates that this is a social-psychological necessity.

It is difficult to have any respect for a dogma which puts making concrete look like concrete above human welfare, quite apart from the fact that reinforced concrete is always a structural lie, unless you regard rust stains as a glimpse of the truth. But in fact there has been an element of untruthful expression in all architecture, as there is in the human body and just about every living thing. The dogma of 'truthful expression' is a nonsense because it is not only inherently impossible to implement but involves the subjugation of human feelings and needs to material appearance.

*The over-emphasis given by art critics to the value of originality should be considered in this context.*

Architecture requires sympathy with, understanding of and satisfaction of the emotional needs of people. All people are different and all communities of people differ. There is therefore no one way to design. The concept of 'one architecture' is a totalitarian monstrosity.

*Architecture must vary from place to place and people to people. This is in the nature of things.*

At this point is it pertinent to move from western to eastern philosophy, to the mandala. The unity of all things is signified by the circle, the image of the universe. Within the circumference there is an infinitude of balanced variables among which are all the aspects of architectural design but the centre is not architecture it is the One, in Christian terms the Logos to which everything else is related. As the individual building takes its place in and so belongs, for better or worse, to the environment, so architecture with its inherent values takes its place, with all the arts and sciences in relation to and dependent upon the centre. It implies the centre but it is not the centre: it can never be total. The architect is a servant not an authority. Architecture is an element not a totality.

*Architectural relativity.*

From a consideration of how people feel about architecture and what it means in their lives it is natural to turn to the question of how people perceive architecture. Much work has been done on the psychology of perception but the conclusion must be that the way we perceive architecture is no different from the way we perceive anything else. Now if we were concerned, as advertising people are, about the effects we intend to create it would be sensible to study perception theory; and if we believed that beauty was an objective quality of things designed, and were concerned about how it is to be apprehended, the means of perception might again be relevant, but if neither of these conditions applies it is difficult to see how the way in which architecture is perceived is relevant to the way in which it is designed.

It is unsound in the arts to argue from effect to cause. Furthermore, awareness of architecture is only partly perception. Architecture affects the senses of sight, touch, hearing and smelling as well as our 'senses' of space, proportion, balance, scale, decorum, relevance and relationship. It is present to our awareness of it in the process of living, in its associations, comfort, convenience, habitability in the widest sense and its contribution to the quality of living. To isolate visual perception of it is liable to be misleading.

If we are to believe that the emotional experience of architecture, the feeling of architecture by people, is related to the total experience of living in, around and with it, the crude simplifications of perception theory, as we know it, are misleading apart from the fact that an affective approach to design is suspect. The whole tenor of our consideration has been that the architect must feel for and with, not attempt to affect. This is perhaps the main warning from experience of modern architecture, namely, that it has tried to affect, to impose rather than understand and interpret.

At the functional level we design for the effects we want to achieve but at the aesthetic level we must allow the effects to come from artistic interpretation not predict them.

Form does not follow function: that is a crude over-simplification. Design transmutes function into art. Art is the exploration, interpretation and transformation of nature through feeling and creative activity.

It is all very well to talk of being sensitive to what people feel but how does the architect set about it, bearing in mind that the communication of feeling is difficult, that many people not only cannot say what they want but do not even know what they want, and that the possibilities available to the creative architect may well be beyond their experience? Psychology can help to some extent but it tends to use data which may not refer to normal uncomplicated people and its generalisations can become a tyranny. Psychoanalysis of every client and user is hardly a practical possibility even if techniques for environmental psychological diagnosis were available. Some generalisations must be attempted, some guide-lines indicated, but they must be flexible and adaptable to every kind of locality and every sort of community.

It might be hoped that folk architecture would be a reliable guide, at least to domestic design, but no folk com-

*Professor Prak's* **Visual Perception of the Built Environment** *(Delft 1977) seems to me to go beyond perception theory into the nature of design for people.*

*cf. R.G.Collingwood cited above.*

*i.e. design which is intended to affect.*

*Interference is not the architect's proper function.*

munity is uncorrupted by outside influences. The Bantu tribesman has notions of a brick house with windows and a corrugated roof; the Devonshire villager may aspire to an 'ideal home' which is a vulgar travesty of the folk architecture of Sussex.

The first question we must ask is a genuinely ethical one. To what extent should the community exercise control over individual designs? Is the Devonshire motor engineer to be permitted to build a red, white and blue concrete filling station beside the village green? Is the French property owner to be allowed to put a twenty-storey hotel beside the Gothic cathedral and is the local governmental authority to be allowed to pull down a Georgian square to build a shopping centre? Freedom of the individual, economic prosperity, the authority of a majority elected without reference to environmental considerations to override even the wishes of its own party supporters, such issues as these, which are moral issues outside architecture, clearly affect the built environment. The barbarians are still with us and there are no simple answers. Most communities, since the onset of industrialism, have been prepared to degrade their environment for riches which, when achieved and amassed, are usually taken elsewhere to some less spoiled place.

On one point practically everybody is agreed: the spoiling is real and does happen. Environments deteriorate, sometimes to the extent of being unfit for habitation or any use whatsoever. Nobody thinks this is good in itself: it is seen as a price that has to be paid for prosperity, employment and the like. It is seen as the lesser of two evils, but there is no doubt about it being evil. The moral judgment is made by society. The architect who goes along with the rape of the environment must know that he is going along with evil. The moral question of whether he should do this on, for example, the excuse that he will do a less bad job than somebody else, is a moral problem for him as a citizen and is outside the scope of this book. The moral dilemma for the architect—and it is all too common in modern society—is 'Can I do a good job in a bad cause?' It is not such an easy question to answer as might be supposed. Some very fine buildings have been made in causes which some people would deeply disapprove.

The proposal to construct a red, white and blue concrete filling station on a village green among the thatched cottages is a moral one for the garage owner, for the village as a community and for the local authority, but it is an aesthetic one for the architect and paradoxically many architects would turn it into a moral problem. If, for example, the planners decreed that it was to be a brick and timber filling station with a thatched roof in character with the cottages then architects

*Devonshire and Sussex are English counties with characteristic and charming styles of folk architecture.*

*Georgian; eighteenth century English style based upon Palladio.*

would raise a *moral* objection—it would be *wrong* to produce a sentimental pastiche; it would be a denial of the architect's right to design according to his own artistic *conscience* and it would be a betrayal of the obligation to build the architecture of our time and reflect in architecture the character of our time. All these are *moral* and rather sanctimonious objections.

It is a bizarre feature of our time that many people concerned with the arts want to impose upon society art which does *not* reflect the realities of our age, as though they were bent upon deceiving posterity and the historians of the future about us! This is a very queer kind of morality. The Victorian period in Britain is often blamed for mixing morals with aesthetics, but at least they were honest about it.

The problem of the red, white and blue filling station remains. Does he please his client and build a horror? Does he do as the planners say? Does he accept the view of the amenity society which points out that there are two filling stations within half a mile and this one is unnecessary, or does he see this as a challenge to produce a design which improves rather than harms the village scene? If he is a good architect one hopes he will, if the job does go ahead, produce the beneficial design but, and it is a very important but, can he be trusted to refrain from moralistic dogma and clap-trap about reflecting contemporary society and design freely in accordance with the genius of the place? Unfortunately, far too often, no; and this is a reason why we have to suffer the disadvantages of bureaucratic control of design.

An age reflects its character in the art it does genuinely and honestly in tune with the people of the time. It is no use pretending. In the context of a theory of architecture it would be disingenuous to ignore this problem but we have to admit that all the questions cannot be answered in terms of architectural theory; they are questions of social ethics and ecological morality.

Within the context of our theory, however, we can say again that architecture is not an expression of the personal emotions of the architect. It is not his ego that he is expressing, nor is any art a means of conditioning people, of affecting their emotions in a deliberate way. It is in the kind of problem that we have been considering, that the architect must 'die to himself' in order to interpret the genius of the place and the feeling of the people. And here we must pass almost into the realm of metaphysics, because in the relationship of place and people, 'people' are not just one generation deep. We may or may not practise ancestor worship, most of us don't; progressives and people on the make may alike scoff at tradition, but in fact any community is an organism and when we build we are relating past, present and future.

*Architecture is not an expression of personal emotions of the architect. It is the exercise of an artistic skill in the service of people.*

If we look at the phenomenon of architecture in the way in which we have been trying to understand it we may now begin to relate inherent properties of architecture to the feelings of people.

The Earth is where we live, we are creatures of the surface of the Earth. We have nightmares about falling from heights and about being buried under the surface or drowned in water. We have deeply subconscious fears of height and depth, which it is adventurous to overcome, but our natural habitat is on the surface of the Earth where we can walk about. Our myths of paradise envisage a pastoral landscape or a garden.

Innumerable excuses may be made for suppressing our instinct; excuses based, for example, upon population statistics or the ambition of architects to build towers; but the instinct is there because we are what we are, creatures who walk about on the surface of the Earth.

We come into being, as the result of copulation, after a relatively long period of gestation during which mother and child are at risk and need protection. From birth we have a long period of childhood and are dependent for a much longer time than other mammals. We have much more to learn and for those who become architects the learning period is very long. Procreation and education can be institutionalised but whatever theorists may decree for other people hardly anybody wants this for themselves. The normal and instinctive way of life in which our natural and uncorrupted feelings are rooted is the making of a home on the surface of the Earth and the rearing of a family. Some people are celibate, through choice, conviction or circumstance, but the roots of their feelings are not necessarily different; and some form homosexual unions which often conform to the normal domestic pattern of making a home. There are polygamous and polyandrous *ménages* but these only require variation of the internal planning. And there are nomads, Bedouin and Gipsy for example, but they also make a nest, a tent or caravan, on the surface of the Earth and try to establish territorial rights.

The natural habitat has space round it or, in some communities, enclosed by it—a *patio*. The natural human nest is a building to enclose space and a territory which is open to the sky. The little hut, the *aedicule*, is not only the primitive architectural solution of a basic human problem, it is also an enduring symbol for a continuing necessity.

But it may be objected that the separate dwelling with its own territory had to be abandoned centuries ago and is totally irrelevant to modern architecture.

The main constraint was the need for security. Defensible space had to be communised and in an age of predatory

*Towers are for defence, for prestige or the signification of aspirations. The natural habitat of man is on the ground. The surface of Earth is the habitat of man. He retreats to towers under restraints.*

*The social base-line is a cottage with a circumference of land. The standard of living achieved by any society should be measured against this. The dweller in a city tower block may well be living at a poorer standard than the less opulent peasant in a primitive hut in an underdeveloped region.*

*For the nomad these are grazing rights. The peasant and his successor, the industrial worker, are progressively less demanding but they still require space.*

*Space is the birthright of people. If a man and a woman generate a human being this is a commitment to its sharing the available space.*

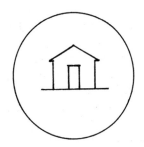

pitched battles, when open towns were sacked, walls had to be built and siege warfare necessitated ever stronger defences within which towns became congested and high rise building, not only of homes but of workshops and even cathedrals was the solution. But it came about gradually and people adapted their way of life. The typical old European city had tall houses with shops, bars, restaurants, workshops at street level and a congenial pattern of living, with a great deal of eating and drinking out of the house, generated a vivid earthy life at street level. This has been threatened and sometimes destroyed by motor traffic with consequent decay of the viability of the town economically and socially. Inflation of land-value and expropriation by developers have forced people out and the dreadful mistake has been made of building high-rise housing without the ground-level facilities which make it acceptable. The *aedicule* remains a starting point for consideration of design for people. We may not be able to build like this but if we take it as a standard and a basis we can think clearly and feel sympathetically about necessary variations from the standard.

Relationship to the Earth and all the deep associations which go with that relationship are still basic to architecture; so is the home.

If high-rise building is necessary it is more sensible to use it for places of work than for family homes. For a minority, adolescents, social nonconformists, bachelors, criminals and the promiscuous, the anonymity of the apartment block has its advantages, but it is still at its best when socially related to the ground, and it is difficult to create the social-commercial base, thriving very largely upon family businesses, artificially. It takes a long time.

Earth-relatedness is a primal emotional consideration in architecture.

Balance, as we have seen, is a more than terrestrial phenomenon. Balance implies repose, calm, peace. Imbalance implies the opposite, activity, movement, conflict. But in living most of us want a balance between balance and imbalance. We have a physical and mental need for some sleep and though complete calm may be preached by some *gurus* most of us, while valuing peace and calm require activity also and the spice of contention. But what of architecture? Generally the requirements for home are peace, comfort, quiet, privacy, freedom from stress. If this norm is to be varied we should ask why. Some people may want their homes to be ostentatious, aggressive, eccentric or status-symbolic. This when recognised as a variant becomes part of the architectural problem of interpretation and like the red,

*Modern appliances such as lifts (elevators) and fork-lift trucks make changes of level in industrial processes relatively easy.*

*High-rise housing requires ground floor commerce on equitable terms. This contradicts the view that commerce exploits society. In fact society may often need to encourage local commerce by subsidising ground-floor rents.*

white and blue filling station, a subject for social-ethical consideration.

Generally in architecture it would seem that balance is to be sought, balance in the design and in its relationship outside itself. Imbalance prompts special scrutiny.

But balances are not individual: they are, as has been said, multi-dimensionally related. We must be on our guard against such fallacies as that 50 per cent gourmands and 50 per cent starvelings is a 'balanced population'; that one hectare of noxious industry and one hectare of park is balanced land-use or, that most troublesome of heresies, that good and evil balance (that God and the Devil are equal and opposite powers). Neither life nor architecture can be based upon isolated equations.

Proportion in architectural design has been shown to have functional, structural and ergonomic roots from which we get preferred shapes and sizes, but a 'sense of proportion' must apply to the whole concept of every architectural design. It is a feeling for what is appropriate. It is closely related to that guiding light of mid-eighteenth-century architecture, 'good taste' and it requires a close *rapport* between architect and client which is by no means easy to achieve when a sensitive architect believes his client to be a vulgar pig, or when the cultured client sees his architect as a venal charlatan!

In practice, however, the problems of appropriateness, proportion and taste arise seriously in the relation of the building to its environment. If an impotent tycoon wants to decorate the inside of his house like a sultan's scraglio that is his affair. If he wants a mini-Taj Mahal in Bath or Nancy the idea should receive sympathetic consideration. Much worse things have happened. In fact all architectural ideas should receive sympathetic consideration. Incongruity should not be decided by puritanical dogma. There has always been an element of the theatrical in architecture from the medicine man's hut to the State Capitol at Washington and the UNESCO building in Paris. It would be a pity to lose this. Proportion in architecture allows for exaggeration of scale and idiosyncracy in a conformist context, as good cookery allows for spice, and music allows of dissonance. Unfortunately, however, these judgments which require the nicest discrimination are now almost universally entrusted to dull servants of the rule-book or flash-harries on their way to public honours. In fact control is no substitute for good architects, but it is part of the price we pay for bad architects and corrupt developers; for the prevalance of environmental immorality.

Proportion in actual building is most important in the size of buildings in relation to each other. Size gives emphasis.

*Wit and good humour are not inappropriate. In some contexts they are desirable. A good example is Port Meirion in Wales by Clough Williams-Ellis.*

Emphasis without meaning is a form of madness which is endemic among planners who use tower-blocks for accents in a plan. Anything big is an environmental bully to which the natural response, in the absence of real admiration on other grounds, such as respect for a cathedral as such, arouses feelings of dislike and resentment. Buildings which dominate, like people who strive to impress, are seldom respected. Harmony can be seen as the reconciliation of challenge and response, not as compromise. As every musician knows, harmony is *not* the same thing as compromise!

A difficult problem of our time is that whereas in the past people who had money to spend on building were well aware of their place in the 'pecking-order', and the architect was asked to sympathise with individuals, the modern scene is full of committees and boards of anonymous and often insecure people. It is almost impossible to feel-with a collective client. There is much to be said for the delegation of authority to a single official, the Clerk of the Works, with whom the architect can establish a personal relationship. Much of the anonymity of modern architecture results from the anonymity of the client. It is no use giving full responsibility to the architect and letting him feel for himself. Bi-polarity is essential to the creation of architecture. This has always been so and is part of the nature of architecture as we have come to understand it. It is an architectural fact of life.

In the actual practice of design harmony is a concept which refers to a great variety of elements. Conventionally in music it refers to consonance, but in a wider sense it embraces many other musical qualities, timbre especially. In architecture, as in music, contrast is a part of harmony; a bassoon contrasts with a harp and a violin with a trombone in harmony. In architecture colour, texture, shape, softness, hardness, reverberation, are all relevant to harmony.

Generally the feeling is that architecture should be peaceful and harmonious.

*As in medieval architecture..*

## 6  INFLUENCES

### FASHION

There has been a fashion for believing that architecture is or should be independent of fashion. This would make it different from the other arts and out of touch with the characteristic behaviour of mankind, for men, unlike other animals, enjoy variety. This is a symptom of the nature of man as an improving animal, a creature which is constantly seeking new and better ways. In mythology this fact is

*cf. Allsopp, B. Civilization—the Next Stage Ch. 14.*

symbolised in many legends as, for example, the story of the Garden of Eden or of Pandora's Box. Not all change is improvement and we are becoming more aware of this fact, but man has this instinct for change which is harmlessly and charmingly expressed in change of fashion. Much of the delight in architecture comes from its responsiveness to the fashion of its period and this is so firmly established as a principle affecting all artifacts that archaeologists and historians confidently utilise stylistic evidence for dating.

The architect has to be on his guard against mistaking fashions in architectural morality among architects, for the real fashions of the world outside. This is another case of the fallacy of treating artistic matters moralistically to which we have already referred. To play its part in the healthy development of society art must not be restricted by moralistic dogma: it must be aesthetically responsive. Only so can it reflect society instead of being an inward-looking and probably sterile cult.


## TECHNOLOGY

Until the industrial revolution architectural technology changed only slowly. Structural design reached an apogee in the fourteenth century and the Renaissance saw lessening concern with technical virtuosity in favour of deliberately simple structural forms and the development of applied decoration, including the orders of architecture, which often masked the structural forms.

Modern technology, furthered by modern selling techniques, has presented an enormous array of new constructional methods and materials. Architects, being human, improving animals, as we have said above, and susceptible, quite naturally, to the surge of fashion for new lamps rather than old, have chosen new ways in preference to old. Many of these preferences have been justified: many have led to structural failure, unsatisfactory appearance or high maintenance costs. Furthermore the excitement of novelty did for a time distract the minds of designers from quality. Equilibrium is now returning and 'gimmickry' is going out of fashion. In architecture, as in mathematics, there is much to be said for clarity and simplification. Technology is a servant not a master, and not a plaything for architects.

*Elegance is the refinement achieved by simplicity.*


## DECORATION

Modernism made a distinction between what it called 'applied decoration' and 'the natural beauty of materials' used in the design. The former was 'false' and 'bad': the use of materials because of their decorative qualities was 'good' and 'true'. Thus a wall of random rubble or fair-face brickwork was good and true while panelling, wallpaper or tapestry were false and bad, irrespective of whether the use of stone or a brick wall of high quality bricks was appropriate for an internal partition. It is easy to be misled into taking this far too seriously. In fact it was a simple matter of fashion—of fashion identifying, in its usual fickle way, for a brief time, with modernism. The internal wall of fair-face brickwork is no more true than the internal wall plastered and papered; in fact, because the simplest and cheapest internal wall is hardly ever made of bricks or stone the block partition, plastered and papered, is more acceptable by purely utilitarian standards than the wall of natural stone or brick.

It has also been said that materials have their own morphology, which means that they are supposed to lend themselves to certain shapes rather than to others; but consider the handle of a chisel. It can be made of beech, ash, boxwood or plastic but the shape of chisel and handle derive from the way it is handled by the craftsman, not from the material. At the practical level of designing a tool for a job, form does follow function but the handle may be red, yellow, blue or green or printed with a pattern of moss-roses without in any way affecting the utility of the tool.

Modernism reacted against the corruption of decoration in the late nineteenth century. This corruption was, to a large extent, but not entirely, the result of the new possibility of reproducing decoration mechanically, but mechanical reproduction geared to good design has fulfilled Morris's dream of well designed fabrics, carpets, papers, clothes and indeed many conveniences of life which he never imagined to be possible. *Such as washing machines, food mixers and TV sets.* Decoration is an essential element in the design vocabulary of architecture. It takes six main forms. These are:

(a) The pleasing qualities of the material used in building. Thus, for example, stones and timbers are chosen for their appearance as well as their structural utility.

(b) Mouldings, from a simple plinth or panel mould to a full classical cornice or the complex subtleties of a Gothic pier.
Mouldings are the punctuation of architecture. They are not arbitrary, any more than commas or points in a sentence, and paragraphs in an extended piece of prose.

(c) The making of transitions between differing materials, between one structural element and another, most notably between a column and a lintel and at points of movement or vibration. The capital and the cover mould are archetypical of this kind of decoration.

(d)   The giving of emphasis without increasing size or proportion. Drawing attention to a main entrance, for example, without making it larger than is functionally necessary.

(e)   The giving of appropriate significance to a building, often by the use of symbols or architectural metaphors. Under this heading come mosaic floors, luxurious hangings and rich carpets, also the hygienic appearance of a hospital or the deliberate austerity of certain types of religious building, and similarly penitentiaries.

(f)   Purely for delight.

## SCULPTURE AND OTHER WORKS OF ART

It is important to distinguish between architectural decoration, such as mouldings, patterns, symbols and conventional representational or abstract devices, on the one hand, and original works of art on the other. The former may properly be designed by the architect, the latter only if the architect is also a sculptor, painter or the like. Works of art are more than decoration and may be an integral part of the building, as notably in Greek, Gothic and Baroque architecture; but they can only be achieved as works of art if there is freedom for the artist to work as such and not merely as an executant of something 'architect-designed'. There is, however, a corresponding obligation upon the artist to accept the architectural context and work as a member of the team.

*It is an impertinence for an architect to 'design' sculpture.*

Much of the best architecture in the world, both east and west, has embodied the work of artists, including architects, working in harmony with each other. The concept and acceptance of format is vital in this matter.

## ECONOMY

Some people think it is virtuous to be economical. If resources are scarce, an economical design may be required. This is relevant whether we refer to the financial resources of a client or to global resources of a material. But here we are making ethical judgments. We may disapprove of extravagance but it is a fact that many admirable buildings have been deliberately extravagant. Gold, a scarce and expensive material, has often been used in architecture for its beauty and its costliness: likewise rare and precious stones, costly coloured glass and finely wrought materials of all kinds. Economy, in this sense of the word, is irrelevant to architectural quality except that it may make it more difficult to achieve.

Economy, in another sense, is part of the actual technique of architecture. Design decisions have to take cost into account. At one extreme a gold-plated dome is out of the question on a nursery school and, at the other, rough-sawn spruce boards are not an acceptable floor for the children's classrooms. Ruskin said 'When we build, let us think that we build for ever', but in practice the architect has to balance capital costs against probable maintenance costs. It is part of the design process to make a sensible *economical* decision. The cheapest solution may often be the worst and least economical.

But there is a third meaning of economy which is of much greater aesthetic significance. This is economy of means for achieving ends. Mathematicians are familiar with the concept of the most elegant solution of a problem. Elegance consists in the simplest possible expression of an idea or argument, one which is devoid of irrelevancies or redundancies. A structure may have this kind of elegance which is evident in some modern architecture and was apparently admired by thirteenth-century ecclesiastical architects in France and England. The most economical solution structurally may, in fact, be very costly financially. Precision is usually more expensive than the rough-and-ready. But many other factors operate against the elegance which comes from structural economy. Among these is the necessity for fire-resistance. The most economical structure would normally be excessively vulnerable to fire. This factor alone excludes the architect from some dimensions of design which he must resign to the sculptor who, in turn, has to work within practical limitations of size.

It is part of the human condition that the best we can do is to achieve excellence within the limits of what is possible.

# 2

# PART  2

# PART 2

# SUGGESTIONS

From consideration we pass to suggestions. They may be thought of as a theory but not as conclusions. Conclusions suggest finality; finality spawns dogma and dogma generates its own refutation. Architecture is an old art which has gone through many changes and remained architecture. It will be enough to see what it is in our time and leave the future to make up its own mind. So what follows are not rules; they are theoretical suggestions about how we may be better architects and explain ourselves to people.

*In order to maintain their character as theory they must remain generalised. They are about architecture as such and not about the practice of architecture in any specific place or manner. The use of THEORY in PRACTICE is to clarify what the architect is trying to do, not explain the technique of doing it.*

I    *KINDS OF ARCHITECTURE IN MODERN PRACTICE*

There are five kinds of architecture, related to each other but emotionally and originally different. A sixth kind is emerging with promise for the future.

1.1    *Folk architecture* is the architecture of people. It has evolved with people in communities and has often been the work of their own hands. Its characteristics are cherished and imitated long after the original determinants of a folk style have become irrelevant.

1.2    *Vernacular architecture* is the result of acceptance by architects of the criteria of folk architecture as a way of design. It is a way of continuing established values in a modern context.

*This is no more 'sentimental' than the printing of sagas and fairy tales with modern machinery.*

*The term* architect *is here used in the widest, not in the narrow professional sense.*

1.3    *Monumental architecture* has its roots in commemoration of the dead and is by nature honorific. By long established custom honour is paid in monumental building to living people and to institutions. Monumental architecture is for mortals and the dead but it is sometimes used in a religious context when men want to glorify God in architecture and stress the importance of the Church.

1.4    *Spiritual architecture* is directed by man towards the spirit world, the unseen powers, the essences which are not material, the gods, concepts, to God. Spiritual architecture is very ancient and commonly takes forms which are peculiar to the cults with which it is associated. Since cults only very rarely rest upon current revelation and are generally conservative of ancient lore there is a strong element of ritual in spiritual architecture.

1.5 *Utilitarian architecture.* Many industries are still indifferent to the appearance of their factories and company directors who live in elegant homes often see no incongruity, indeed a kind of propriety, in ugly, neglected and dirty working places. This is changing slowly but indicates an attitude to certain kinds of building which was almost universal. Architecture, by implication, is in some sense sacred, if only to the household gods. Building for utility was not architecture. Among the influences which have changed this are materialism and humanism. Both have isolated man from the spiritual and concentrated attention upon quality of living, judged by material standards. The non-spiritual has gradually acquired the nature of a cult, a kind of non-religious religion in that it rests upon a *belief*, which is not a material thing. This paradox has elevated utilitarian building to the status of architecture. Utilitarianism gives prominence to economy of means in achieving ends, on the assumption that the economical deployment of resources makes for higher material standards of living. It is associated with functionalism and socialism. Its creed, which rests upon a moral judgment, that material benefit for people is good, gives it a missionary aspect which operates against folk and spiritual architecture but is ambivalent about monumental architecture. Utilitarianism has to its credit that it has brought the design skills of the architect into a large and growing sector of building activity which otherwise would have been untouched by them. The biggest question is whether it is relevant to the homes of people.

1.6 *Humane architecture.* The utilitarian name for places where people live is *housing*, people do not have homes they are *housed*. They may then make homes for themselves in the housing accommodation but the architecture is seldom on their side except in the provision of utilities. The grouping of accommodation units in large blocks, and oppressive administration operating against any expression of individuality, contrast sharply with the character of folk architecture and village communities.

Renaissance ideas applied to domestic architecture were breaking down by the early years of the nineteenth century. Out of the resultant confusion, and heralded by such designs as William Morris's *Red*

*On the other hand, as Frank Jenkins has pointed out to me, estate agents, especially in USA, sell 'homes'.*

*In Britain speculative builders are often much more in touch with what people want than are architects and it is notorious that homes on a builder's estate are much more desired that architect-designed council houses. They are, in fact, more humane.*

*House* at Bexley, there emerged, in all the developing countries, from South Africa to Scandinavia and Russia to California and Australia, a way of designing architecture which was derived from folk architecture. This could be seen as a return to medieval practice. In such building modern structural techniques were used but the *significant appearance* of folk styles was preserved, giving rise to an extremely varied range of styles, some of which were derived from age-old localised traditions, such as the black-and-white half-timbering of the Welsh marches and others from vernacularisations of renaissance design styles such as English Georgian, Cape Dutch, American and Spanish Colonial and Scottish Baronial. Some of the greatest talents of the late nineteenth and early twentieth centuries were deployed in this designed vernacular architecture. The garden city movement and the growth of landscape architecture upon the sure foundation of the English tradition were closely related. This architecture proved to be exceedingly popular almost all over the world. An immense amount was built. Some of it was badly designed, and speculative builders brought the style into disrepute as they were later to do to the 'modern movement'. Modernists, with their totalitarian and utilitarian leanings, crusaded against popular taste and what they called sentimental design and 'fancy-dress architecture'. Nemesis has overtaken the modernists whose style, as it has now become, is often called 'packing-case architecture' and felt to be boring, overbearing, and soulless. This is a popular generalisation which takes no account of a considerable amount of modern architecture, especially houses, which are charming and humane, indeed it is arguable that just as Palladianism gave rise in England, to vernacular Georgian so Modernism has developed a vernacular form which begins to take its place with the traditional styles.

Comparisons with music are often useful and we may compare this wide-ranging vernacular architecture with modern folk music which comprises traditional true folk music and equally genuine modern folk music related, both to the jazz tradition, with its striking technical innovations, and to modern classical music.

But the desire for a humane architecture is not limited to houses, and whereas the Arts and Crafts

*Architect for the Red House was Philip Webb.*

*A vernacular genuinely based upon new materials but resting upon a very shallow tradition and still lacking some of the basic commonsense of the old vernaculars.*

Movement was reacting against a growing faith in technology, machines, large organisations and various forms of totalitarianism, the current leaning towards humane values is supported by a growing awareness of the ecological condition and commitments of mankind. Instead of being over-against nature and 'mastering' nature it is now fashionable to see man in the context of nature. Survival, it seems, depends upon man being a natural component in the ecosystem. This is a philosophical revolution which has its architectural expression in a series of relationships, the house to the garden, the garden to the landscape, the landscape to the ecosystem, the ecosystem to the Earth as an organism. Instead of totalitarian thinking we have participation thinking; man in relation to the *rest* of nature, not in predatory mastery of nature, set over it.

*Man in the ecosystem.*

*cf.* Genesis, *I, 26.*

One consequence of the modern movement, envisaged but not correctly evaluated by the Futurists, has been the demonstration that man can make a hell on earth not only by neglect of design, as in industrial slums, but also by design in the production of a concrete jungle, a hell of impersonal, threatening, inhuman architecture, in which man feels isolated, anonymous, and frightened; reduced by a totally man-made environment to a condition which is now the stock-in-trade of science-fiction visions which chill the spirit as the ogres, dragons, and witches did in Grimm's Fairy Tales. We have a new admonitory folk-lore to go with totalitarian architecture.

Humane architecture is the opposite of totalitarian. It is undisciplined from outside but not unordered from within. It is inhibited only by the requirements of its nature to be harmonious and congenial. This is an attitude which is applicable to most kinds of design and in practice it requires human scale, relatedness to environment, significant appearance, comfort, adaptability, conformity with the manners and customs of society, and appropriateness to the nature of the user. It is not necessarily refined and elegant: it is appropriate and individual.

*The diseases which most inhibit architects from producing humane architecture are;* arrogance *which is the inability to* sympathise, snobbery *which is the failure to communicate with "ordinary" people and* technical incompetence *which is the failure to be able to do what people need. (This could be true of the other arts).*

Out of censoriousness and rigidity, the imposition of will of the architect, we move towards a sympathetic, accommodating, humane architecture.

2     THE PRESENT STATE OF THE KINDS OF ARCHITECTURE

*2.1*     Folk architecture continues in the old way in some places and even shows signs of revival as a traditional craft-based architecture. The 'architects' are craftsman-builders and their way of working is ideal for small simple communities. Where the tradition exists or is reviving the introduction of extraneous fashions is pointless. But there is also a new kind of folk design which is the direct product of rising standards of living based upon industry. As productivity rises, so industrial wages rise and artisan wages rise in sympathy. The result is that the cost of craft work by building tradesmen becomes related to the general level of wages in industry and maintenance work on existing buildings, which is almost always hand work done by craftsmen, becomes more and more expensive. It is in some countries already beyond the means of the ordinary householder and the implications for the maintenance of the existing stock of not very good quality modernistic buildings are alarming.

For many people the answer has been *Do It Yourself* and this has been helped by greatly improved facilities for teaching handicrafts in schools and the growth of a new retail trade, DIY Supplies. Components are being standardised for DIY craftsmen and practically the whole range of building trades is covered. Socially this incentive to acquire and develop craft skills is beneficial and architecturally it is becoming a force to be reckoned with. It is in fact a return, under modern conditions, to folk architecture and it would appear to be a coming economic necessity to foster this in the maintenance of publicly owned housing. The potentialities, social, environmental and architectural are interesting.

It would appear that architects should begin to concern themselves with DIY maintenance techniques and possibly with design services for the DIY worker. If architects don't somebody else will—indeed they have already started and in Australia, not to mention older countries like Sudan, DIY house-building has long been common practice. The growth of industry and consequent rises in wages are having the ironic effect of forcing people back to folk techniques, and not only in building.

Because of rising maintenance costs high-rise buildings will probably become non-viable in the near future.

Meanwhile, it is becoming apparent that 'simple' communities are still capable of 'beating the system' and restoring the joy, which many people think

*It is also a factor in publicly owned housing tending to. force the sale of such houses to private owners. Indeed rising maintenance costs must eventually depreciate capital value.*

should be part of the human condition, of making one's own nest.

In the more 'advanced' countries architects have succeeded in eliminating much of the joy in building. In this they have been aided by the financial institutions which employ them.

The architect is a designer whose work has to be completed by other people. The architect, like all artists, claims a right to 'job satisfaction'. Many architects make job satisfaction equivalent to artistic integrity. But the other people in building are entitled to job satisfaction and it is not unreasonable to suggest that this should run right through the building process. This must mean design that takes account of the feelings of the artisans who will actualise it.

2.2 Spiritual architecture is becoming polarised. Cathedrals, mosques and other great temples are still being built. They are still, what they always were, offerings in architecture to God, however named and however conceived. Religious wars continue in a few places but there is widespread interest in the great variety of ways of religious experience. Ecumenicalism and humanitarianism in the Christian churches is tending towards more personal involvement, less authoritarianism and a folk character in architecture which is entirely genuine. This links with DIY and the concept of a place of worship built by the community with their own hands is an answer to the lack of provision in 'housing schemes' for the spiritual needs of people. Here again we have the pioneer spirit re-emerging in societies where technology-based industry has priced itself out of the market.

*We have become accustomed to the separation of the spiritual and the secular. It is possible that we are approaching a time when specific buildings for worship will no longer be required, suggesting "not the triumph of materialism but the sanctification of the hitherto profane, the recognition of the spiritual in all the works of man." (Jenkins). This condition seems to have existed in earlier times and appears to be implicit in Minoan architecture.*

Spiritual architecture, whether it be in the simplicity of a Quaker Meeting House or the inspiring splendour of a Cathedral, is architecture which serves human experience outside purely material relationships. It is between man and God, not just for man, and this requires a special kind of sympathy in the architect.

*It is to be hoped that some of the space 'freed' (or to be more realistic, 'sterilised') in high-rise housing schemes may well be used for various kinds of voluntary building.*

2.3 Monumental architecture for the dead is not so fashionable in an age which is doubtful about the future and sceptical about the past but the vogue for materialism, of whatever political flavour, and the strange yearnings of post-classical architects for monumental opportunities, together with lingering inspiration from Futurism and the more extravagant formal visions of Le Corbusier, keep monumentalism

*Rigid attitudes of town-planners tend to inhibit the natural development of communities which may be spiritual in direction.*

alive while commercial institutions, especially those directly concerned with the manipulation of money, such as banks, insurance companies, stock exchanges and finance corporations, continue to like monumental buildings. The idea that architecture should *dignify* the person, people or institution inhabiting the building is age-old and not disreputable, though it may be mildly funny.

2.4 Utilitarianism in architecture is on the defensive. People do now expect from architecture more than the mere satisfaction of functional requirements; and functionalism itself is suspect as an aesthetic, for at least two reasons. First, things which are functional and judged to be beautiful remain beautiful when they are no longer functionally very efficient as for example, a Rolls Royce Silver Ghost; and second because 'useful therefore beautiful' implies a discredited renaissance aesthetic in which beauty is an inherent quality. The main difficulty about utilitarian architecture is that its aesthetic implies a single, once and for all pattern of use, but in fact use changes, the Wesleyan Chapel becomes a carpet warehouse and the cotton millionaire's mansion becomes a borstal. A malt factory becomes a concert hall and a cinema is converted for Bingo. There is something about architecture which is independent of and perhaps superior to functional utility. A medieval castle remains architecture long after gunpowder has destroyed its utility and the Parthenon is architecture even after it has been converted to an arsenal and had its heart blown out. Materialism is a kind of faith but fewer and fewer people actually believe in it.

2.5 Humane architecture is emerging. It is the architecture of the future if we can avoid totalitarianism. It can accept into itself folk architecture and its derived designed vernacular, as well as the new DIY folk tradition. It can be spiritual at any level. It can recognise vanity as a tolerable human foible and go along with monumentalism quite cheerfully. It must recognise the values of utilitarian architecture and seek to improve upon them. In its own right humane architecture is evolving as a new discovery in the development of mankind. It is an architecture of sympathy with people as they are, not as they were or will be and certainly not as any prig may think ought to be, but just the marvellous human race with its splendours and its faults, just as it is.

*It is interesting, as Jenkins has pointed out, that the apogee of monumentalism coincided with the growth of rationalism and materialism, c. 1780-1840.*

*An architecture of sympathy with people as they are.*

3    *THE ATTITUDE OF THE ARCHITECT TO*
     *THE DIFFERENT KINDS OF ARCHITECTURE*

3.1   Much confusion arises from not distinguishing one
      kind of architecture from another.

3.2   In the client-architect relationship which is funda-    *See below, p.87*
      mental to the phenomenon of architecture an early
      clarification can be made.

3.3   Humane architecture over-rides the other categories
      which can become sub-headings.

      3.3 (1)  Folk architecture is by definition humane, but
               being essentially the architecture of small
               communities it can be too rigid and restrictive.
               It is humane at a relatively primitive level of
               social evolution.  Out of folk architecture
               came *designed vernacular* which seeks to
               develop folk styles with the skills of the
               architect.  The fact that it has been used very
               widely for suburbs does not invalidate it. It is
               probably what most modern people really
               want.

      3.3 (2)  Spiritual architecture is not necessarily humane
               at all.  It may be very simple, warm and
               comfortable as in some village churches, but
               it may be deliberately reaching out into a
               spiritual state.  Arguably this is still humane
               but not in the sense that we are using the
               word.

      3.3 (3)  Monumental architecture can be humane and
               easily lapses into sentimentality, but it is
               capable of being assertive, brutal and in-
               human.  Remember, monumental archi-
               tecture is really the architecture of the dead:
               there is an element of morbidity in it when
               it is designed for the living.

      3.3 (4)  Utilitarian architecture has the disadvantage
               of seeing man as a utility. The architect is
               asked to feel with the master over against the
               servant.  It is an architecture for slaves, so,
               while utility, fitness for purpose, is a necessary
               aim, *purpose* has to be seen differently when
               utility is in the context of humane archi-
               tecture.

                 Purpose is always conditioned by humane
               considerations which is certainly not the case
               in a great deal of utilitarian architecture.

## 4  RELATIONSHIPS

4.1   To say that everything is related to everything else and that nothing exists in isolation may be true but it is not very helpful beyond drawing attention to the fact that an architect designs in relationships and every building involves complex relationships within itself and outside itself. Moreover the word *exists* raises problems which, though they are metaphysical, are highly relevant to the practice of architecture.

4.2   Consider a circular disc of white paper. As every draughtsman knows, a circle has a centre. What is it? We may define it in many ways, as the point at which the diameters intersect, the point where the radii meet or in practical drafting terms the point from which the circle is struck with compasses. We can mark the point with a dot, but this is not the centre. It is a smaller circular disk of ink. We could proceed to find the centre of this and mark it with a smaller dot and so *ad infinitum*. The centre does not exist in the ordinary practical way yet everybody knows it is there.

4.3   Likewise we take easily and may use in design the relationship which exists between the side of a square and its diagonal $1 : \sqrt{2}$. The square root of 2 does not exist yet we can use it. It is a relationship not a dimension yet we can turn it into a dimension.

These familiar facts have interested philosophers and artists for centuries but they are mentioned here only to draw attention to the fact that relationships in architecture may involve things which are not in the ordinary sense real. Circularity and centrality are 'things' we can think about in a design context, and we may call them conceptions or abstractions, yet in architecture we are dealing with real shapes, and real people. If there is difficulty in thinking about such apparently simple things as the centre of a circle, how much more difficult is it to think about the relationship between people and architecture. We can think about them up to a point and then let dogma or tradition take over, employ our powers of feeling, intuition and creation, letting reason go as far as it can on the evidence available, then using our creative powers as designers to supply more material for the reason to consider. A sense of proportion is, as most of us know from the practical experience of living, itself a balance between reason and emotion, each monitoring the other.

We should not expect architecture to be easy; part of its fascination is the extreme difficulty of making it simple! Given that it is difficult we should be foolish to neglect the accumulated experience of mankind. If we have a distaste for history we can call history experimental evidence. Examination of it can indicate some of the architectural 'facts of life'. Many are the result of relationships which are hard to identify, others may reveal practical rules or even principles.

5    *THE APPARATUS OF ARCHITECTURE—* Facts of architecture as revealed by experience i.e. continuous experiment over long periods.

5.1    All building rests upon the Earth and the ground must be strong enough to bear the weight of the building without subsidence. Though we can do some things to modify the bearing capacity of the ground, such as excavation to firmer material or piling, the fact remains that the weight of the building must be spread so that the load is nowhere more than the ground can bear; furthermore if the ground is anything but solid rock the load must be evenly spread to avoid the possibility of differential settlement. The load of a building may be continuous or intermittent. Walls generally apply a continuous load, pillars an intermittent load. Usually the weight has to be spread out, according to the bearing capacity of the ground. Greek temples, such as the Parthenon, exposed the spreading out of the foundation but most buildings conceal the fact that there is a foundation and so walls and columns appear to rest upon ground which in many cases could not possibly support them. The Parthenon truly expresses its foundations, one might think, but in fact they are on solid rock and there is no structural need for them. In almost all buildings the appearance of the relationship between the building and the Earth conceals the way in which the weight is transferred.

5.2    Architects have never been concerned to show truth about foundations which are literally the *basic* relationship of architecture to the Earth upon which they stand. In a paved street it is impossible to show

*cf. 'Consciousness can only exist through continual recognition of the unconscious.' Jung, C.G.,* Works *vol. 9, p. 96.*

*The history of architecture is a record of experimental experience.*

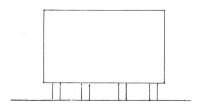

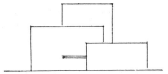

the truth about the foundations and if, in this most basic matter, so-called truthful expression is impossible how can we think it matters further up the building? Almost all buildings rest upon a visual deception about their relationship to the Earth.

5.3   *The enclosure or definition of space.* Walls and columns rise from foundations to enclose or define the limits of a space in the horizontal plane. All architecture is either continuous wall or intermittent supports. The wall may be five metres thick and made of granite blocks, or it may be a skin of transparent glass or plastic. Intermittent support in the form of columns indicates an enclosure of space but allows for interpenetration, for outside to become involved in inside and for inside to merge into outside. But wall may be pierced by windows and intervals between columns may be filled by wall, transparent or otherwise. The basic elements of horizontal definition are vertical walls and columns supplemented by windows, which approximate towards columnar design, and screens which approximate towards mural design.

5.4   Enclosure is completed by roofs which, being the boundary between the architecture and infinite space, having nothing to support but themselves, are the most variable element in building and have provided the most exciting opportunities for the play of architectural creativity in design. In folk architecture they are generally the most characteristic and recognisable feature.

    Roofs can be flat or steeply pitched. The flat roof has been characteristic of warm countries where it can be used as a terrace but it has, even with the most modern techniques, the disadvantage of being difficult to make waterproof, and any failure is liable to be more damaging than it would be in a pitched roof. Pitched roofs traditionally overhang the walls and protect them from rain. The protection afforded diminishes proportionately to the height of the building but because the damage water can do increases with the height of the wall, eaves or cornices are still a valuable feature making for durability and lowered maintenance costs even in high buildings.

5.5   All roofs provide insulation. Some roofs, mainly pitched roofs, enclose space which may be used. Devices such as dormer windows and the mansard

*Walls and columns support the roof. The 'roof over our heads' is a basic human requirement from architecture.*

*Overhang and overlap are two of the soundest and most basic devices in architecture.*

*The overhang or eaves of a roof is the origin of the cornice; the protected gable-end, of the pediment.*

roof give a mural function to parts of the roof. The designer may usefully clarify in his own mind the distinction between a sloping wall and a sloping roof.

5.6  Most architecture involves enclosure. This is of two kinds; enclosure of space and enclosure of territory. A room is an enclosure of space, a *patio* or terrace is an enclosure of territory. Enclosure of space creates a difference between inside and outside. To avoid ambiguity anything with a roof is inside, anything without a roof is outside. Thus a courtyard is outside and a loggia is inside. Territory is enclosed by anything which visually separates it from other territory; a wall, hedge, fence, parapet, or even a ditch. An open colonnade or pergola is not considered an enclosure. Occasionally enclosure of territory is effected but the eye deliberately deceived as with a ha-ha, an electrified wire or a beam of light.

5.7  Enclosed space always modifies climate. Enclosure of territory usually modifies climate and this is a factor to be taken into account when designing. Climate varies from place to place and seasonally. The moderation of climate for the benefit of people is one of the principal purposes of building. Folk architecture is not exclusively determined in its form by climate and available materials but most folk architecture is suitable for the climate of the place in which it is built. It is useful evidence.

*Micro-climate.*

5.8  Suitability to climate is determined by judgment and requires a nice balance related to climatic extremes, human comfort, the properties of materials, capital, maintenance and energy costs. Near the equator extremes are between night cold and day-time heat. In high latitudes they are between summer warmth and winter frost. Altitude, shelter, air currents and proximity to water all modify climate.

5.9  Climatic territories generate appropriate ecosystems and an ecological approach to design would suggest that architecture should be in harmony with the ecosystem.

*Climate is a major influence on design.*

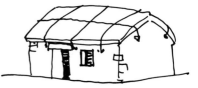

5.10  The practicalities of designing for people who have a social pattern of living in a climate indicates that architecture would naturally vary from place to place. The experimental evidence of tradition supports this view. In alpine valleys for example, micro-climate can vary from approximately mediterranean by a lake to sub-arctic no more than two kilometres away on the mountain. Valley-bottom architecture is different from mountain-side architecture. Under the influence of Modernism and the totalitarian idea of one architecture, stylistic similarity was imposed on all architecture, using energy-consuming technology to maintain comfort. A high price to pay for stylistic conformity.

5.11  *The humane approach to architecture requires design for people in climate.* Given these two variables, people and climate, plus the originality of the architect, there is infinite scope for variety in architecture. This is confirmed by the built evidence.

5.12  The first condition of architecture is structural stability.
The second condition of architecture is that it be weatherproof.
The third condition of architecture is moderation of climate for the comfort of people.
The fourth condition of architecture is that moderation of climate be achieved with low expenditure of energy. (This is an old condition dictated by scarcity of fuel but exacerbated in modern times by extravagance in the use of finite resources).
The fifth condition of architecture is economy in the use of scarce materials, such as metals.
The sixth condition of architecture is durability and low maintenance costs, bearing in mind the extreme costliness of fabricating standardised parts which have gone out of production.
These are all practical matters of common sense in proceeding with the design of a building for people. We now turn to more difficult things.

*Conditions of architecture 1 to 6.*

6  THE STATE OF MIND

6.1  The phenomenon of architecture is a development of the phenomenon of man.

6.2  In the short time he has existed it may be that man has evolved very little biologically but the accumulating efforts of his mind have created a body of mind-experience which passes from generation to generation, continuously renewed and enriched.

6.3    The accumulated experience of architecture is part of the mindsphere. It contains design experiences which have stood the test of time and passed into the collective consciousness.

*Mindsphere, or, as Teilhard de Chardin called it in* The Phenomenon of Man, *the* noosphere.

6.4    Among the recent entrants to the mindsphere is the idea of there being a collective unconscious. The roots of this may go back beyond the emergence of man from the rest of the primates. Feelings about territory, height, balance, security, weather, water and fire, must be deeper than architecture but we shall not attempt to separate conscious and unconscious influences in the human mind.

*See; Jung, C.G.,* Works *vol. 9, p. 10.*

6.5    It is suggested that our modern minds are conditioned in ways of thought and feeling about architecture by accumulated awareness which goes back, in part, beyond the beginnings of man as a species. While it is not necessarily impossible or wrong to de-condition our minds in some respects, and in fact the mindsphere is continuously evolving, the architect endeavouring to design has a sufficiently difficult problem and might well accept the present state of mind as a base-line. We shall do this in trying to indicate the nature of architecturally relevant phenomena in the present state of mind.

7    *RESPONSIBILITY IN DESIGN*

7.1    The proverb 'People who live in glass houses should not throw stones' has a double meaning. Firstly, glass is easily broken, so do not encourage people to throw stones by throwing them yourself or, by extension, if you are vulnerable be careful whom you attack. But the second is more subtle and more relevant to architecture. Glass is transparent and a glass house lacks privacy so, having no means of concealment you are at a disadvantage compared with your neighbours who can keep their secrets in houses with solid walls. Occasionally glass houses have been built as follies, or conceits, or in order to enjoy a beautiful situation where privacy is otherwise secured.

7.2    One thing we require of a home is privacy. Enclosure is not only required to create a suitable internal climate: it is required to give privacy. It is not a matter of certain constants being the reason for requiring privacy: feelings vary and to some extent are conditioned by up-bringing and social usage. (In some places people are shy about pissing, in others they think no more of it than a cow does.) Privacy is required as such, privacy to be alone, or alone with one's mate, or with one's family or to do something which one wants to keep private. Rationalise how you will, the instinct is, at least in a great many people, for privacy as such. People don't put net curtains to a window twenty floors up in an isolated tower block in case someone with a telescope in the next block a mile away might be looking! It is not rational, it is a feeling for the comfort of enclosure. It *can* be rationalised away but it is not for the architect to say it *should* be.

Deprived of home privacy and cut off in cities from the seclusion of country places, courting couples now make love in public, creating an illusion of privacy for themselves by the magic of their relationship or, put more mundanely, by pretending the public is not there. Man is an adaptable species but there is no reason why architects should exploit this. Privacy is desirable, not always easy to achieve, but not lightly to be sacrificed.

*Privacy is also a practical necessity for many activities such as preparing for examinations. Acoustic privacy may be even more important than visual privacy.*

7.3    Most people have had dreams about falling, flying or levitation. We are told that these have origins older than man. Fear of heights is common; a compulsion to fall is not unknown and man is, in fact, a creature of the surface of the Earth, being physically adept at walking and running about. Climbing, despite his monkey ancestry, is strenuous and he can't compare with a fish at swimming. For flying he needs elaborate apparatus to which he trusts his life.

7.4    For the normal business of living man is most at ease on the ground.

7.5    In modern conditions where people go out to work it would seem best to give priority to homes in proximity to the ground and use high-rise techniques for commercial, business and industrial premises.

7.6    Sleep is essential and there is a subliminal need for security. This is satisfied by 'going up to bed' or putting shutters on windows and bolts on the door. For some people this becomes a neurosis but it is probably true of most people that they want some concession to security as well as privacy in a sleeping place. The behaviour of many animals confirms this.

7.7 Fear of fire may be less ancient in origin, but is very real and perhaps worrying to architects more than other people for whom it is more generalised than specific to a particular building. Death by fire is horrible and the architect's heightened awareness of the danger may indicate the need for sympathy with other people's phobias, some of which he may not share. Fire regulations may sometimes be stupid and a handicap to the designer but fire has always been a notorious hazard in buildings and it is irresponsible to ignore it or get away with minimal provision.

*Many architects instinctively assess the fire-risks and escape exits before settling down for the night in a strange hotel. Some people in high-rise housing have to live with a constant fear of fire.*

*Here we touch upon a* genuine *moral obligation. cf. p.10*

7.8 All our subliminal and conscious fears are capable of developing into neuroses. The architect cannot be expected to design for neurotics unless he is specific-ally required to do so, but to design, for example, a deliberately vertiginous building, with parapets half a metre high, for architectural effect, is irresponsible. Phobias are a reality among the other realities which the architect has to resolve in making a design.

*Phobias are real.*

7.9 It is suggested that *the seventh condition of good archi-tecture is a responsible attitude towards fears and dangers.* Responsibility has an ethical and not merely a legal meaning.

*The seventh condition of architecture.*

7.10 Irresponsibility begets regulations and legislation which, when all is said and done, are a poor substitute for good design by architects.

8 *ARCHITECTONIC ARCHETYPES*

8.1 The mindsphere, conscious or sub-conscious, contains archetypes, images, proved solutions and experience-based preferences of an architectural nature.

Long before the first architects, we may suspect that man was habituated to the idea of *significance* in things. He might call this significance a spirit which was something that existed and had power but was not material. Two levels of existence were apparent, the material and the spiritual. Of these the consensus of ancient opinion was that the spiritual was far more powerful. Frequently the material object became a symbol for the spiritual power.

Modern man may reject such ideas as primitive though he lives in a world where men are moved and profoundly affected by powers such as Christianity, Communism, Patriotism, Loyalty and Solidarity which have no material embodiment except in symbols.

Early man discovered, as every child re-discovers, that it is all-but-impossible to draw without meaning. Cave paintings exemplify the marvellous skill generated in the recognition of the power of the graphic artist to symbolise the bridge between the material and the spiritual worlds.

8.2    It is uncertain whether spiritual, folk or monumental architecture is the earliest. We do not know whether man made tombs or votive erections to spirits before or after he first identified himself with the building of his home. We do know that cave-men consecrated caves to spiritual powers but neither the domestic cave nor the cave-temple became an archetype. The archetypes that did emerge were the standing stone, the mound, the trilithon and the *aedicule*.

*But it is arguable that some temples (perhaps Romanesque cathedrals) are artificial caves.*

8.3    The erected stone is an obvious way of marking a place as well as an obvious fertility symbol. The mound is an obvious way of marking a grave as well as the symbol of a breast, and so of maternity and the mother goddess. Neither of these is particularly relevant to architecture in our time. But the *aedicule*— the primitive hut—is a valid symbol for modern man. As Noah's Ark it is the house placed on a boat to save what was good in the world from the anger of God. All the animals, male and female, two by two, were saved in the ark. Two linked together became the archetype of survival. The trilithon, that is two stone columns yoked together by a lintol, becomes both the symbol of survival of the race, through regeneration and fertility, and the symbol for ancestry, for memory. It replaces the primitive symbol of the phallus, the obelisk, the pillar, by a new awareness of the duality of human origins.

*TRILITHON and AEDICULE*
*See also Allsopp, B.* Towards a Humane Architecture *for a fuller exposition of these concepts.*

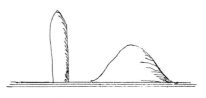

8.4    To the modern pragmatist it may seem that what happened six or seven thousand years ago is irrelevant to the modern architectural problems. This is like suggesting that a plant has nothing to do with its roots and a child nothing to do with its parents, but it is a fact of life that a plant cannot grow without roots and everything, including ourselves, is the potentially fertile end of a series of genetic relationships which goes back to the emergence of life on Earth.

8.5 Before man there was no architecture. Architecture is an epi-phenomenon of man. Without man it could not occur and it has to be considered in relation to man. This is important because for architects to dedicate themselves to architecture is only a second-hand dedication to man.

8.6 The *aedicule* is the archetype of the house. It emerges in very early times as a form which has three elements within an environment. These are the *room*, the *porch* and the *roof*. The room is the personal or family sanctuary. The porch is the transition to outside, the roof keeps the rain out and makes enclosure. A territory is the buffer between the dwelling and the outside world, a place where children can play, herbs be grown, wood chopped and stored, or pets kept, *as of right*. It is significant that in the pre-industrial age size of territory was the major determinant of rank.

*Names of the European nobility were territorial, e.g. Duke of Northumberland signing himself Northumberland; von Wittelsbach, de Guise etc. Even Bishops signed with the name of their see and still do.*

8.7 The trilithon does not enclose space. As a portal it can be taken into the *aedicule*. As a porch it supports the gable but these are functional uses. As a *symbol* it can be free-standing or linked in a colonnade. As the triumphal arch it is supported by an arch, as a structural device, but remains a lintol carried by two piers. It is stable and exerts no lateral thrust. It is the basic element of monumental architecture and the Romans, for whom monumental architecture was part and parcel of a way of life, preserved the pure form in the design of important temples. Arches were permissible in mundane architecture and good enough for emperors!

*It was in Gothic architecture that the arch came into its own as a major element in an architecture of equilibrium.*

8.8 The idea of a foundation is developed into the form of the altar, a raised podium for a holy practice. The setting of something upon a pedestal is an ancient symbolism of importance like the raising of the hands of the priest in prayer or offering.

8.9 Steps lead up to a pedestal or down to a crypt. Ascent or descent are deep significances in architecture. Steps are symbolic, as well as practical.

8.10 The single column is the pole of the tent, the symbol of paternity, the support of the roof, the patriarch. We cannot begin to understand the history of architecture if we think the column is just a structural expedient.

8.11 It is possible to cut oneself off from the inherited and the subliminal meanings but these are in everyone. The architect can only cut *himself* off, not other people, and if he does so it is at the expense of sympathy. He is discarding the deepest responses in those for whom he works and with whom, in architectural terms, it is his business to communicate.

8.12 We need more knowledge, study and awareness of the architectural psychology of people. This is not perception theory or anything so superficial: it is the deep instincts of man for architecture which, in those who become architects, is the foundation upon which they will build their education and practise their art.

8.13 It would be foolish to pretend that it is not a mystery; but it is a mystery to be explored, not explained away.

*It can be said that all science is exploration within a mystery.*

8.14 Some people have what we call a *gift* for music. This seems to be an emphasis of something which, in less degree, is present in most people. Likewise in architecture, some people have a special gift, but the appreciation of this gift by people is possible because they share it in less degree. Buildings are not meaningless or irrelevant to their lives.

*In the making of a home everyone participates in architecture.*

8.15 The artist is not a special kind of man. He is an ordinary man with a developed human faculty in the group of activities which we call arts. As Ananda Coomaraswamy said, 'Every man is a special kind of artist'. For an artist to despise the public is like a fish despising water.

*Ananda Coomaraswami in* Man and the Transformation of Nature in Art.

8.16 *The necessary understanding among architect, client, and public depends upon a basis of common feeling which is deeply rooted in mankind.*
*This is the eighth condition of good architecture.*

*The eighth condition of architecture.*

## 9    FUNDAMENTALS OF DESIGN

9.1   One, two, three, many. Most of us nowadays have learned to count up to ten after which we start again. (In English eleven and twelve take us up to the dozen and give us a glimpse of a duodecimal system, but this has not yet matured. Anyway, we represent eleven as one-one and twelve as one-two. In fact we count up to ten and start again.)

9.2   But in sight and sound one, two, and three are the easily recognised numbers.

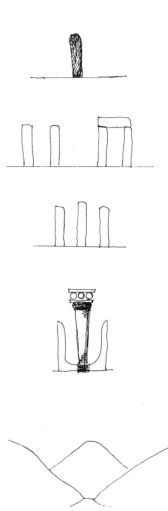

9.3   Unity is alone, the death knell, the single drum beat, the obelisk and also the phallus. Death, commemoration and generation. It is also the centre, the One.

9.4   Duality is *yin* and *yang*, left and right, the march step but in music we write it in four time—left right, left right—indicating continuity. We have an intuition which physics confirms, that duality is fundamental to the universe. It is divided yet related like the horns of a bull—or a dilemma, yet two together make a pair which we can see as separates in a unity—a divided unity.

Three is magical. The Trinity, the resolved duality, the circular motion of the waltz, the triad, the trilithon. Two brought together by one.

9.5   Fundamental to architectural design is that we look at one, go between two and are drawn towards three.

9.6   In terms of recognition four tends to many and repetition, confusion, or breaks into two twos. Five resolves into two twos about a centre, six is on the edge of monotony, that is the repetition of one.

9.7   We are familiar with the idea of rhythm in music and recently we have become aware that some 'primitive' people can make and appreciate very complex rhythms and give them significances. In visual patterns also 'primitive' people have explored ordered complexity especially in the making of rugs. Rhythm is grouping and repetition, and psychologists are beginning to explain some of the ancient insights in terms of gestalt psychology. What is much more important, however, than how we perceive is

61

what we mean, what we intend; and if we are to proceed psychologically we must pursue research at deep levels of feeling, motivation and intention.

9.8 All honest art is made *from* the artist *out* to the beholder to 'say' what the artist has to 'say' not merely what the recipient wants to hear. This is why artists must ignore critics. The artist is not a magician, he is an honest broker of his own feelings and insights.

9.9 Rhythm is a basic element of design. It has been much neglected in modern architecture. How many facades are an endless repetition of crochets!

9.10 Proportion is relationship. It rests upon what we rightly call a *sense* of proportion and this varies from person to person and time to time. But the variation is within socially acceptable limits. On the edge of the limits we may find genius and beyond that madness. Disproportion in architecture is not advantageous unless, perhaps, it is the result of genius in the architect.

9.11 People expect architecture to look *in proportion*, but for the architect proportion permeates every aspect of design.

9.12 There is, however, a group of relationships which are architectonically important. This group can be divided into three categories.
  1 The internal volumes of the building, in themselves and in relation to each other.
  2 The outward shapes of the building—massing.
  3 The design of the surfaces of the masses.

9.13 Traditionally proportion has been considered in terms of numerical ratios the validity of which was believed to have been established by, principally, a misleading analogy with acoustics. As a result ratios were thought about arithmetically instead of in areas and volumes. Up to a point this did not matter because linear ratios, such as 1:3 in the proportion of a window, did define a rectangular shape without fixing its area; and the idea of a plan—the nave of a church for example—being three squares long and one square wide as a result of employing 1:3 could be made volumetric by a height ratio of 1:1 giving a triple cube as in many sixteenth-century churches.

*cf. note on page 28 about N.L. Prak's work in this field.*

*Rhythm, contrast, balance, proportion, harmony and other qualities which we should expect to find in architecture are exemplified in music. There is no doubt that they can exist and no reason why we should be deprived.*

*(Opening of J.S. Bach's Concerto in D major for piano, flute and violin.)*

The disadvantage was, however, a very serious one. Architects were made to think in lines which would never exist except on the drawing-board, instead of in surfaces and volumes which would be the actual forms of the buildings. Futhermore, proportion without dimension could appear to validate major proportional discrepancies in area or volume. There was therefore no satisfactory relationship between proportion and what architects call *scale*. In terms of renaissance proportional theory something could be 'in proportion' but 'out of scale'.

9.14 Reduced to its simplest form the renaissance theory of proportion (Alberti) *was x : y is good where x and y are both whole numbers* or *one of them is to the other as 1 : $\sqrt{2}$*. The alternative in fact invalidates the proposition, being, as Alberti himself said, a mystery. Numerous attempts have been made to extend renaissance proportional theory but all rest upon two fundamental fallacies. The first is renaissance cosmology which, in ignorance of the effects of motion, relativity, complementarity and the nature of matter, constructed a mechanical model of the universe which is entirely wrong; but harmony with this untrue universe was the basis of the theory. The second was the notion that beauty is an absolute quality of things and this is no longer tenable. Theories of proportion rest upon the assumption that architecture can be made objectively beautiful by the use of them and this is not acceptable.

9.15 Because of the second fallacy, stated above, it would seem to be useless to try to re-establish renaissance aesthetics upon a basis of modern physics.

9.16 Yet we would be foolish to discard the renaissance achievement as being useless. All human decisions and practices have been, and continue to be, based upon incomplete and partly wrong information. The subliminal feelings we have considered in 8 above are not negligible because they arose from deep superstition. In an organic world, of which we are part, the upper branches of a tree do not invalidate its roots. The fallen leaves renew the topmost twigs. The Renaissance is within historical time but it has already become part of the sap in the system, part of our mental and aesthetic heritage. It invented a way of design which was commodious, firm and delightful within its own terms and remains delightful for us long after its theories have been dissolved and its function departed. How is this?

9.17  Proportion is a matter of judgment, part of the creative process of designing. It must take into account all the relationships in and around a building. It includes harmony, rhythm, meaning, micro-climate and all the parts of the building in satisfactory relationship. And if we ask what may be *satisfactory*, the answer must be *satisfying to human beings in the context of their own time*.

9.18  But is there any basis upon which we can make decisions about proportion, bearing in mind the question we have asked? How is it that Renaissance, Greek and Gothic buildings which were designed to rules which we no longer accept are still considered, in their different ways, to be beautiful, even in ruin and when they have no function? An answer may be indicated in the concept of *format*.

## 10  FORMAT

10.1  The word format is most commonly used in publishing books. The format of a book has to be decided at an early stage. This is a decision about the shape and size of the book as, for example, *Crown Quarto, 128 pages* which is the format of this book. Commonly authors have some notion of the ultimate format as they begin to write. Though the Concise Oxford Dictionary limits the word to 'the shape and size of a book' we shall extend it to any art form because there is no other word for what we mean and the absence of a word suggests a new insight.

10.2  The common word *form* is far too wide and confusing in its meaning. We are concerned with size, shape and, in an artistic sense, structure; how the work is arranged and put together.

10.3  In poetry the sonnet is a format, the size and structure are predetermined. In music a sonata is a format. Sonnets and sonatas may be good, bad or indifferent: there is no presumption that the format will determine the quality any more than the book format *Demy Octavo* guarantees a good book or gives any indication of subject-matter.

10.4 In literature we have such formats as novel, novelette, biography, monograph, encyclopedia. In poetry, lyric, sonnet, epic, saga; and in music, prelude and fugue, toccata, opera and all the dance formats.

10.5 A Bach Gavotte does not cease to please as music when the dance goes out of fashion.

10.6 In architecture, as in muisc and literature, there are many kinds of format. They can be classified as follows:
   (a) Formats of function.
   (b) Formats of design system.
   (c) Formats of style.
   (d) Formats of pattern.

10.7 *Formats of function* The format is indicated by the building type, such as hotel, church, factory, house, town hall, museum. Given the format the architect investigates the social norms for the type. A hotel in a small town in France, for example, is different in character, in requirements and in social uses from a comparable hotel in England or California. The conventions of a Catholic church are different from those of a Protestant church. The factory regulations in one country are different from those in another.

10.8 *Formats of design system* There are many different ways of designing, among which the renaissance proportional system, modular systems, and 'kit of parts' systems may be mentioned. If, for example, the Palladian system of design were accepted as a format the architect would learn the system and apply it to the programme. In this particular system function is subordinate to dogma and the range of design decisions to be made by the architect is narrowed within very strict conventions. Likewise in pre-fabrication systems the architect works within strict limits imposed by the system.

*But whereas the old formats, like Palladianism, had been perfected by the experience of many artists over a long period, prefabrication and other modern formats are still very crude.*

10.9 *Formats of style* Styles of architecture are the end-products of extensive building experience, within a definable society, subject to physical restraints of climate, technique and materials and in accordance with the culture and value-systems of the people. The roots of style are frequently in folk architecture, but major political, cultural and economic changes can and frequently have brought about changes of style.

Fashion has also effected changes from a style which became boring to a new style, simply for the sake of change. Even the 'modern movement,' which originated in and was committed to a rejection of style, produced a style upon which fashion and other influences worked for change. In the wake of the 'modern movement' it is difficult to be dispassionate about style but it is a phenomenon of architecture, whether moralists approve of it or not, and the question is arising, whether in extending a 'modern' building of distinction, such as Le Corbusier's *Pavilion Suisse*, stylistic conformity is desirable or not. Certainly from the thirteenth century onwards architects have been aware of the problem and there is a long series of examples of keeping in style, of accepting a stylistic format. In recent years most architects and students have been committed to a single stylistic format. If a stylistic format is accepted it becomes necessary to learn the rules of the style. In some cases ('François Premier' and 'Modern' are examples,) this can only be done empirically. In the Palladian style, which resulted from an aesthetic-system format, the rules are known.

*As, for example, Mannerism in 16th century Italy and Art Nouveau c. 1900 in Belgium, Scotland etc.*

*e.g. The continuation of an 'Early English' triforium in the 'Decorated' nave of Beverley Minster and the 18th century 'Tudor' style additions to Hampton Court by William Kent.*

10.10  *Formats of pattern*  Patterns are of two kinds, natural and imposed. Natural patterns are typified by the crystals in a snowflake or the ramification of a tree. The crystals assume, according to atmospheric conditions, innumerable hexagonal symmetries of design, each of which is a natural pattern, though no single snowflake is exactly like another, the possible arrangements within natural law being infinite. The ramification of a tree is the resultant of directional growth in variable atmospheric conditions which also exert directional, but variable, stress upon growing shoots. Furthermore the tree grows and ramifies according to its genetic structure. We are only just beginning to be aware of the natural patterns which affect architecture. Decisions, far from being free, are always and inevitably made in context and every decision affects the context of the next decision. There is thus an element of natural pattern in all architectural formats. Imposed pattern is much more simple and is illustrated by the format of symmetry which, though it occurs in nature in a vast variety of manifestations, is consciously selected as a format by architects. Once chosen, it imposes its own discipline, the normal formula being symmetry on one axis.

*'W.A. Bentley photographed more than 4000 different snowflakes and believed that he'had barely broken the surface of possibilities. It could really be said that no single snowflake is exactly like any other.' (G. Seligman in* Chambers Encyclopaedia, *London 1959).*
*If the format of a crystalline hexagonal disk is so flexible no architectural format would seem to impose unbearable restrictions upon design!*

*Architects, in recent years, have been influenced by 'computer thinking' which has been based upon two-value logic and leads to the 'critical path' method of analysing problems. The danger of this is that there is no way of recovery from a mistake at any point and in a subject where many value judgments have to be made the process is limited and often misleading. Reference may be made to* How a Computer Should Think *by A.D. Belnap in* Contemporary Aspects of Philosophy, *Ed. Gilbert Ryle, (Stocksfield 1976).*

This is a format without being a design system and it is independent of style. It is often considered to be arbitrary and un-functional, but consider a snowflake.

10.11    In the two post-war periods (1919-39 and 1946-69) which cover the two phases, initiation and consummation of Modernism, architecture was polarised to *totalitarian world-style authoritarian architecture* on the one hand and, among a great many architects who practised in what they believed to be the one style to end all style, a deep concern for their own *individualism* (not other people's!)    The polarisation of *totalitarianism* and *self-expressionism* is characteristic of the age out of which we are moving towards awareness of the urgent need for *balance* and the rejection of the authority of the architect 'doing his own thing' over-against society. We may hope thus to emerge from the architecture of war-neurosis.

10.12   It is necessary at this point to stress what a study of history makes apparent, the fact that every period contains within itself the seeds of the next and that a great deal that has been going on in architecture since 1946 is transitional towards a humane architecture. Naturally it has been despised or ignored by the pundits of Modernism. Historically it will be of enormous interest.

10.13   Format involves acceptance of limitations.  In the mood of self-expressionism limitations were disliked by artists. But most of the greatest art has been produced within limitations. The sonnet, the fugue the sonata have not inhibited great artists from doing their best. The acceptance of limits within which a work must be done, whether the format be stylistic, systemic or functional, provides a challenge to which the artist can respond. The discipline of working within the limits, even apparently arbitrary limits, facilitates concentration upon meaning, significance and the minute examination of every detail which makes for the quality of unity which was one of the main aims of the renaissance architect. The recognition of a format by the public is an aid to understanding.

10.14   Format helps to concentrate the creative mind upon essentials.  Choice of format is a matter of judgment and generally an appropriate subject of discussion between architect and client.

*10.15* Environment is an important factor to consider in making a choice of format. Once the choice is made the format imposes a discipline which helps the architect by channelling decisions into a range of compatible choices.

*10.16* There is need for study of formats as such and research on these lines could help to create common ground between architects and planners.

*The study of formats, both comparatively and inventively, could be a very important element in architectural education.*

*10.17* It is possible to describe a format without making any design commitment, just as it is possible to say the format of a poem is to be a sonnet without any commitment to language or subject. An architect may have a preference for one or more formats over others just as some composers like to write opera and others prefer concertos.

*Developing countries need to create their own appropriate formats.*

*10.18* An architect's character is revealed in his preference for formats. Some are bombastic and like always to make 'the big statement', while others like to work in miniature. The public's taste for architects is probably like their taste for other kinds of people. Neither the big-mouth nor the niggler is particularly popular. There is no need to quarrel with public taste in this.

## 11 QUALITY

*11.1* We can now take the concept of format back to the consideration of enduring quality. Format is a frame within which quality can be achieved. Looking back over the past we can recognise formats in which it was achieved but what is the common element in good architecture?

*11.2* There is only one formula which applies to the Palace of Minos, the Parthenon, the Maison Carrée, Sancta Sophia, Autun Cathedral, Chartres, the Taj Mahal, and so on up to the present day. It is that in each age architects of genius were able to bring together and crystallise the achievement of their people. These great works were never prototypes, never original. They came like fruit when the tradition was ripe for them.

**An example of a mature format. Tiene Palace at Vicenza by Palladio.**

*i.e. When the Format had been perfected.*

*11.3* This is cold comfort for the architect, or any artist, who works when the time is not ripe, but this is a fact of life, just as it was bad luck for the mammoths of Siberia to be caught in the advancing ice. Architecture is a phenomenon of man and reflects his condition, but in the ups and downs of civilisation where does the individual architect stand, is he pushing down or up? Is he cynically retreating into self-satisfaction in his design or even into purely mercenary practice? Is he with the demon or with the spirit of his age.?

11.4 Quite simply this is a question of faith, of faith not in architecture but in man.

11.5 There is no formula of design which will achieve greatness in a building. The best an architect can do is the best that is possible for him in his time and this may be recognised (but probably won't) as a step towards the masterpiece two generations later.

11.6 Supreme achievements set standards but a plant does not normally derive nourishment from its flowers.

*There are exceptions; carnivorous flowers which 'eat' flies.*

11.7 There is consolation for architects in the fact that the Parthenon had to wait until the late eighteenth century for full recognition of its virtues.'

11.8 Any artist who is trying to produce a masterpiece is allowing his attention to wander from his work. The best anyone can do is his best.

11.9 The only person who can know whether he has done this is the artist himself and he is often unsure. He can know whether he has tried but he cannot know how much he has achieved.

*The best service which critics can render is to recognise and encourage excellence.*

11.10 It is one of the few disadvantages of historical study that some architects—and other people—become preoccupied by concern about their future place in history.

*In other words they want their work to be monument. cf. 'exegi monumentum aere perennius' Horace Odes III, xxx, I.*

## 12 ACCUMULATED LORE

12.1 We have recently become used to the fact that the Earth goes widdershins, that it spins anti-clockwise and so the sun 'rises' in the east. We know that the sun does not *rise*, that its apparent clockwise motion is our anti-clockwise motion. The moon, however, goes round us. It also rises and sets. The terms *rise* and *set* are accepted, not because they are true but because they describe appearances. In this most fundamental matter, the rotation of the Earth on its orbit round the sun, upon which all life on Earth depends, we organise our lives upon the appearance not upon the fact. Until about five hundred years ago (an infinitesimal amount of time in the history of the universe and not very much even in the history of man) the apparent reality conditioned our minds. Since the truth, or what we take to be the truth, was revealed, we have not made any adjustment and we should not applaud any fanatical, puritanical evangelist of science who asked us to call sun-up, *earth-down*, and sunset *earth-up*. We might even remind him that cosmically there seems to be no such thing as up or down: he would only be substituting one relativity for another.

12.2    Whether we think cosmically or biologically the essences established by errors are, within limits, true. The goddess Athena may be a figment of the imagination, but the culture which grew around this figure was not only true but enormously powerful. Athena was powerful even if she did not exist.

*It is tempting to say, 'therefore she existed'. It depends upon what you mean by* exist.

12.3    Similarly, the patterns created by renaissance aesthetics have not died. The foundation upon which they were raised may have been insecure but the architecture of the Renaissance, or any other period which created fine buildings are part of the heritage.

12.4    Reform is not achieved by cutting off roots. It is doubtful whether cutting off heads helps either.

12.5    Given that all experience is founded upon, at best, partial truth, what has been accepted from the past into the mindsphere has validity.

12.6    The awareness will vary from place to place. Toronto will be different from Tibet. The inheritance is likely to be local and cultural. But given the phenomenon of the Renaissance, an area in which what is called '*western architecture*' has been practised has a common classical tradition, with local variations. Behind this lies Gothic architecture. Neither of these great systems of architecture lacked discoveries of lasting, perhaps permanent value.

*From the seventh century onwards the Byzantine version of classicism began to develop as Islamic architecture. Many of the qualities which we call classical achieved new and splendid formats in Islamic civilization.*

12.7  *Classical architecture* flourished in Greece and Rome for a thousand years up to about AD400 and was then revived in the fifteenth century to last until modern times when many of the principles of classical design were absorbed into what was called the 'modern movement'. Discarding the theories upon which this system was founded, the most important results which have passed into the mindsphere are as follows.

(a)  The ideal of wholeness expressed in the dictum that good design is that to which nothing can be added and from which nothing can be subtracted without disadvantage.

(b)  Recognition that a building has three parts, base, accommodation and roof, each of which is an essential element and is defined by horizontal mouldings.

*Plinth, String-course, Cornice.*

(c)  Acceptance of the orders of architecture as fully evolved, fundamental components of design; these also having three component parts defined at the points of change by mouldings.

*Base, Shaft, Capital.*

(d)  The use of mouldings to define the conceptual parts of the design and effect transitions.

(e)  Consistency of material and the avoidance of distraction by change of material, colour or texture from the consistent geometry of the design.

(f)  Consistency of proportion in the relationship of all the parts to each other and in the differentiation of the social importance of the various parts of the building.

*Commonly the first floor was the* piano nobile. *The ground floor was for services, the top floor for servants and dependants.*

(g)  Dignity and decorum. Grandeur if it was appropriate.

(h)  A hierarchy of scale, with, despite humanism, spiritual architecture at the top, then monarchy, nobility, wealth, civic, gentry and clergy. This order changed with the Industrial Revolution and the growth of capitalism.

(i)  A hierarchy in planning based upon axial arrangements of rooms in order of importance and a sense of procession in three dimensions.

(j)  The alternation of light and shade and the sculptural modelling of interiors in an ordered and rhythmic way.

*The* Beaux Arts *formats are still worthy of study if only because of their mastery of the alternation of light and shade.*

(k) The recognition of architectural design as an intellectual discipline and the reasonable expectation of intellectual as well as aesthetic appreciation.

The design-system of classical architecture, in its various forms, has been expounded in many books to which reference can be made. For the architect who wishes to build classical architecture, it is essential to study the system in depth, not merely to imitate. Classicism as practised in the eighteenth century is the fruit of two millennia of experience.

12.8   *Gothic architecture* has commonly been supposed to be totally different from and opposed to classical architecture, but this is a myth manufactured in the renaissance period by protagonists of the Renaissance. Truth was further obscured in the eighteenth and nineteenth centuries by the legend that Gothic architecture was *romantic*, which in its revived form it sometimes was, but not in the middle ages when it was at least three different kinds of architecture, namely, *functional defensive architecture* in castles and town walls, *spiritual architecture* of extraordinary quality in churches and cathedrals, and a highly developed *folk architecture* in houses, farm buildings and such factories as there were in those days, most notably wind and water mills. Three kinds of architecture were able to flourish side by side and have distinct stylistic characteristics, folk architecture especially being immensely varied, and much of it, right up to modern times, directly derived from Roman architecture. This was in Italy, southern France, parts of Spain (and in the early middle ages probably over most of France and western Germany). Medieval military architecture was a great improvement technically upon Roman, mainly because of necessity. Spiritual architecture in western Europe, evolved directly from Roman over a long period of church building, but outside Italy little remains of the basilican churches of the so-called Dark Ages during which, under the auspices of the monasteries, the technical and agricultural developments which made a new civilisation possible occurred, and the military technology which saved nascent European civilisation from being engulfed by Islam took place. About AD1000 a reinterpretation of Roman architecture, based upon masonry instead of concrete, occurred in

*Folk architecture developed into vernaculars of great beauty and sometimes of great complexity flourished in the late medieval period and persisted during the Renaissance and right up to modern times when it linked to the Arts and Crafts Movement. The vernacular tradition rooted in the middle ages was more significant than the so-called Gothic Survival.*

the building of monasteries, and later of cathedrals, on an unprecedented scale, producing eventually, at Durham, the structural break-through which made Gothic architecture possible—the ribbed vault.

Throughout the Romanesque and Gothic periods Roman architecture, the orders and, apparently, Vitruvius were known and the geometrical disciplines of classical design were, in common with the Latin language, studied and developed. To the purist the Latin language was debased, just as English has been debased in becoming international. To the strict classicist Roman architecture was debased but in fact the Gothic architecture which emerged in the twelfth century extended classical theory and structural technique far beyond anything the Romans had ever done, and in spiritual architecture, dedicated to something very different from the mundane observances of pagan Rome, produced an architectonic system which might be considered to make the Parthenon, superb though it is within its own terms of reference, look like a smooth version of Stonehenge.

The lessons for us of Gothic architecture include:-

(a) The possibility of different architectural systems operating simultaneously to serve the various needs of a society.

(b) The etherial possibilities of geometrical systems of design.

(c) In spiritual architecture, the possibility of buildings which punctuate and glorify external space while at the same time creating transcendental internal spaces which are the counterpart of the external space.

(d) If the simultaneous achievement of optimal internal and external design in the definition and enclosure of space were taken as a standard of excellence in architecture, no architecture ever produced anywhere could compare with European Gothic.

(e) The most subtle expression, in structural form related to mouldings, of the *linear* concept of forces in structure.

(f) In ecclesiastical architecture and heraldry the best that has been achieved by man in the relationship of colour to significant symbolism.

*The ribbed vault rather than the pointed arch (which was not uncommon in Romanesque architecture) is the distinguishing characteristic of Gothic architecture.*

*All the surviving early texts of* De Architectura *are medieval. The book was evidently a standard reference in monastic libraries.*

*i.e. various formats.*

*In medieval thinking, the House of God in the likeness of Heaven.*

(g) The use of structure as a language for poetry.

(h) In folk architecture, the most precise and the most comfortable reconciliation of built form with social status.

(i) In military architecture the last architectural interpretation of chivalrous war before the cannon heralded the atomic bomb.

12.9 *Islamic architecture* In the seventh century after Christ the Prophet Mohammed inaugurated the major challenge to Christianity as a religion which offered mankind a communal form of worship and an individual relationship with God. Islam came out of the desert with no architecture and assimilated the Hellenesque architecture of the eastern Roman Empire. What was begun under Constantine and achieved under Justinian in Hagia Sophia reached its ultimate fulfilment in the work of the Armenian janissary (under the Turkish Sultanate) Sinan the Great (1489-1588). This Levantine Sir Christopher Wren produced a vast number of buildings, but the Mosque of Sulieman the Magnificent is his greatest work and perhaps the outstanding architectural achievement of Islam, though there are many competitors for this accolade. Islamic architecture is the direct heir, through Byzantium, to ancient Greece and its supreme achievement is in the development of the dome, but it is also the prime exemplar of abstract architecture at a level which makes modern western abstractists look childish. For more than a thousand years, of which the first nine hundred were one of the most creative phases in the history of architecture within the Islamic sphere, architects, the roots of whose techniques went back to ancient Sumeria and the origins of astronomy, practised under a religious prohibition of representational art. By western standards this was a terrible deprivation, but westerners have come to an interest in abstract art and it is well to acknowledge that they come new to something which Islamic artists have explored for centuries. What Islamic architecture can offer now is experimental evidence of exploration in the field of pure architecture. Is pure architecture humane? The answer might be no, but let us be careful. The typical Islamic home is one of the most beautiful and commodious in the world. It is arguable that people take the place of images and Allah takes the place of

*Hellenesque is the eastern equivalent of Romanesque. The term was first used by W.R. Lethaby. It includes Byzantine and Islamic architecture.*

*The corbel dome was pioneered in Greece c. 1400 BC but not developed by the Greeks until c. 330 AD.*

*Hagia Sophia (Sancta Sophia) in Istanbul, the Church of the Holy Wisdom.*

*Byzantium was re-named Constantinople, the city of Constantine, in the 4th century.*

idols. The reasons are religious: the results, whether we look at houses or mosques, are architectonic and they are for people according to their way of life and their beliefs.

(a) Islamic architecture rivals Gothic in the relationship of inside and outside, in the transformation of space, not transcendentally, as in Gothic, but abstractly, creating not an atmosphere but an essence in its own right.

(b) Islamic architecture inherited and amplified the Byzantine genius for treating surfaces in architecture. The best example is the Taj Mahal.

(c) It is supreme in the West in exploring the possibilities of linear and coloured decoration in natural and artificial materials, and especially ceramics.

(d) It was extremely successful in the controlled design of internal space.

(e) No other architecture (with the possible exception of Minoan) has been so successful in controlling internal natural lighting and ventilation. It is a marvellous exemplar of non-energy-consuming control of internal climate.

(f) As might be expected in an architecture derived from ancient Greece, it excels in the proportioning and modulation of architectural form and in refinement of detailing.

(g) It achieves, not least in domestic architecture, an extraordinarily successful synthesis of structural form with humane requirements whether at the level of spiritual devotion or domestic comfort.

(h) It achieves an admirable balance between decoration and plainness, and the decorative treatment of functional elements.

12.10 *Scenic architecture* The idea that architecture provides the scenery and sets the stage for living is very old and certainly goes back to ancient Greece, to the Agora and the Acropolis. People of the Middle Ages had a great sense of pageantry not only in regal and military settings but, as can still be seen in such cities as Siena, in the festivals and junketings of

*A valuable and intimate study of Turkish domestic architecture is* The Coral Buildings of Suakin *by Jean-Pierre Greenlaw (Oriel Press, Stocksfield 1976).*

citizen-craftsmen and merchants. The village green or open space, the world over, is likewise the setting for a way of life. Some of the most splendid 'theatres for living' were created under the influence of the European Renaissance, the Piazza di San Marco at Venice, the Piazza at Vicenza with its Loggia del Capitano by Palladio, the Scala di Spagna in Rome and that most theatrical of settings, the Piazza di San Pietro in front of St. Peter's in Rome.

Islamic architects created marvellous settings combining architecture and landscape gardens as at Fatehpur Sikri and Agra. China and Japan, as well as fabulous Tibet and the ancient civilisations of America; delighted in setting the stage for life to be lived according to the standards of their cultures. So widespread is the evidence that we must believe this use of architecture to create scenery is a fundamental human activity. This is what people expect of architecture.

Baroque architecture in Europe and America turned away from the precise geometry, and the isolation of the single building inherent in renaissance practice, and used architecture to create an appropriate setting for a new way of life, the pompous and ceremonious life-style of seventeenth-century 'Society'. Baroque architecture, whether we see it in the courtly settings of Versailles, Leningrad, Nancy and Caserta, or in the pompous monasteries of Austria and Germany, such as Melk on the Danube, is frankly scenic. But Baroque is only appropriate to a particular and peculiar life-style which, in the period under consideration, pervades Church and State while excluding, except as respectful admirers, all the lower orders of people.

Rococo art coincided with the growth of the 'polite' class of people and, not unnaturally, was long seen as the debasement of nobility. But the pompous Baroque scenery became distasteful, even to monarchs such as Louis XV of France. The Petit Trianon prepared the way for the rustic and romantic *Hameau*.

The scenic attitude to architecture split in two after the decline of the Baroque. One was towards elegance and prettiness, sensibility, charm and delicate delight, the other was towards romanticism, and both ways paid a great deal of attention to the growing fashion for what we now call easel pictures. Classical architecture and landscape were reinterpreted by such artists as Claude de Lorraine. In England

*Baroque architecture did not abandon geometry: it made it three and four-dimensional to create scenic effects of great depth and complexity (cf. contrapuntal music).*

*The picturesque hamlet built at Versailles for Marie Antoinette.*

especially, Gothic architecture was looked at afresh with romantic eyes. But far from being, as is often suggested, an aberration, Gothic Revival architecture was a logical development of the idea that a *scene* could be conveyed in a *picture*. People began to see architecture and landscape in terms of pictures rather than in terms of parade grounds, (military or ecclesiastical).

The eighteenth-century picture had a frame. People began to look at nature in terms of framed pictures. In the west we coined the word *picturesque* for a kind of awareness which Chinese and Japanese artists had been exploring for centuries. Quite suddenly the West became aware of the art of the East.

Two-dimensional pictures, painted or photographed, can properly have frames round them, but there are no frames round architecture. We are on-stage, in among it.

The lessons of scenic architecture are important.

(a) Architecture does provide the scenery for our lives, and scenery affects the way we live.

(b) Scenery helps to create an atmosphere. It may be respectful or frenetic, cowed or complaisant, but what architects design does affect the way people can live and feel.

(c) Under modern conditions, with an expanding population and a diminishing need for people as functionaries, the quality of living of those who are not 'necessary' becomes increasingly dependent upon the quality of the environment, upon the nature of the stage on which we play our parts.

*We are having to come to terms with the fac[t] that there are more people than 'we' need!*

(d) These parts decrease in functional importance with two important results. Firstly, the ergonomic efficiency of man becomes less significant as technology replaces labour; and second, leisure, which used to be the prerogative of the rich, becomes available to an increasing number of people. The challenge is for the common man to live instead of being a slave (wage-slave or chattel-slave is irrelevant, but in the past chattel-slaves were generally better cared for, being property, than wage-slaves in some so-called free societies).

*This theme is elaborated in my* Civilization— the Next Stage, *previously cited.*

(e) Aristocratic societies such as existed in Russia, China and Europe created the architectural scenery which was appropriate to a privileged way of life. This was marvellous scenery.

*It is only fair to say that the 'common people' could share in enjoying it.*

(f) If privilege is extended do we perpetuate the scenery of squalor or do we believe that the common people are now heirs to the quality of living, including the quality of environment, hitherto reserved for the aristocracy?

(g) The message of scenic architecture, whether it be Baroque, Rococo, Romantic or Pictorial is that, from ancient times, it has been possible, with sufficient privilege, to set human life in a scene which was congenial, enjoyable and deeply satisfying. This is something neither Gothic nor Classical architecture, as such, ever attempted to achieve.

*It is arguable that egalitarian regimes should do all that is possible to retain the achievements of elitist regimes which were, in a sense, the achievement of those who were exploited. It would be a pity if they had suffered and laboured in vain. The proletariat has a debt and an obligation to its ancestors.*

(h) The idyllic environment has proved to be a realisable dream; it therefore sets a standard against which the conditions in which most people live can only be regarded as a lamentable failure.

(i) It is for society as a whole, through its political systems, to decide what it wants to do with the best its architects can offer to it.

(j) The social obligation of architects would seem to be to tell people how good the environment could be rather than give them the best they can for the money made available.

(k) The great architectural insight of the post-renaissance period has been the realisation that architecture can create the conditions for a much better quality of life.

(l) Without the scenery the play cannot be performed. Architecture is important.

*Metaphor must not be stretched too far. A Shakespeare play can indeed be performed without scenery because poetry speaks to the mind's eye. It sets the scene which the technical resources of the 16th century could not represent; as in* Macbeth,
　*'This castle hath a pleasant seat; the air*
　*Nimbly and sweetly recommends itself*
　*Unto our gentle senses.'*
*The poet uses his art to create scene and atmosphere knowing that these are implicit in the fact that 'all the world's a stage'.*

12.11 *Other architectures* Enough has been said of Renaissance, Gothic, Islamic and Scenic architecture to indicate that many other systems of architectural design, produced by long-established cultures, have qualities the study of which can only enrich the architect's powers of sympathy, understanding and design. Some of these architectures, in Tibet for example, have no connection whatsoever with European classicism yet they are manifestly relevant to any consideration of quality in architecture. The factor common to them all is folk architecture from which they have all arisen. None can be fully understood without knowledge of its folk origins and this is true even of western classicism.

12.12 We are obliged to ask ourselves whether what has happened to man in the last hundred years or so can validate an architecture which does not have roots in folk experience and sympathy with people.

In all humility we, who are heirs to an age which dedicated itself to the exploitation of nature, the acquisition of riches and the supremacy of a material standard of living, should not fail to respect the achievements of other men whose ideas and ideals were different. If we are to move towards a better way of life which acknowledges both the gains and the failures of industrialism and exploitation, we may need to look for standards outside and unachievable within the terms of our materialistic preoccupations. We may also need to rewrite history, not least the history of modern architecture, in the context of a humane system of values.

But if we do this, it is well to remember that only in our age is it possible to contemplate such a system. Progress is not an illusion but the seeds of it are widely scattered over the centuries.

12.13 Modern people are becoming more aware of the architecture of the past as an irreplaceable part of the present environment and as something we have in trust. It is natural for people to make comparisons and to expect to find in modern architecture at least the qualities they find in historic architecture. It is reasonable to expect that the architect will know at least as much as the layman about historic architecture and indeed help the layman to widen and deepen his understanding and appreciation of all kinds of architecture.

*For architects to neglect history is to lose public respect.*

# 3

# PART 3

# PART 3

# THE ACTIVITY OF DESIGNING

*1*     *MAN AT THE CENTRE*

*1.1*     We may admire a design without knowing who did it, but if we want something designed we must start with a designer.

*1.2*     The designer is creative: this implies activity directed towards the production of a design. But activity alone is obviously not design.

*1.3*     Design is not mere repetition, though the word is sometimes used as if it were.

*1.4*     Design involves origination. It is impossible to design without being original, so preoccupation with originality as such is a designer's neurosis.

*1.5*     A distinction is often made between *art* and *design*. This is fallacious, but so firmly established that we have to accept the usage which distinguishes certain kinds of design as being art. This leads to unfortunate misunderstandings about art which it is inappropriate to discuss here except to say that it is impossible to produce any work of art without making aesthetic (that is based on feeling) decisions about arrangement of material, whether the material be musical sounds, words, lines, colours or building materials.

*1.6*     In all art there is making with material and there is decision-making.

*1.7*     It is arguable that decisions can be made without feeling. A computer can make decisions and produce an artifact. The computer has no feeling and cannot produce a work of art. But a computer has to be programmed by a person who makes judgments which may be based on feeling. It is conceivable that a computer can be *used* in making a work of art. A computer, at present, is a tool for making very rapid decisions according to a simple system of logic. But we do not need a computer to make 'logical' decisions and people tend to assume that the kind of reasoning we employ in making logical decisions is the best way of making decisions. For many practical purposes logical reasoning, with or without assistance from machines such as computers, is very useful and sometimes enlightening. But what we have accepted from the last two and a half thousand years as logic is now itself under assault and is recognised as being a very primitive and clumsy tool for thinking, so clumsy that it is like using a screw-driver to perform a brain operation! Lateral thinking, which is a new name for something architects and military strategists, among others, have had to do for centuries, is still tied to two-value logic though it has the advantage of bringing arguments along, side by side, with an awareness of their effects upon each other.

1.8    But in art we make decisions in parallel and in series while a faculty of our minds continuously relates and balances intention with what is happening in the process of creation. Thus, a painting is made with sensitivity to what has been already done, to the feeling of the artist both for subject and medium, to the structural organisation of the picture, which may have been partly predetermined, and, most marvellously, a recognition of something which will only exist when the picture is complete though it is not a picture in the artist's mind which he is, so to speak, copying onto his canvas; it is a *foreseeing intuition of a completeness which is only in process of creation.*

*The reality of artistic creation goes beyond the present limits of understanding.*

1.9    Much more might be said, and has been said, on this subject, but here it is sufficient to note that the artistic activity is more like the growth of a plant or animal from a seed than any process of logical thought which we can even imagine. And if we continue to think in terms of a genetic analogue we may notice and refer back to the concept of a format in comparison with a genetic pattern. The genes decide what kind of plant a seed will produce, but cultivation is extremely important, whether it is the 'cultivation' provided by the ecosystem (and this is ruthlessly selective), or the care of the gardener.

*The seed knows what it is to become. To say it is programmed raises an enormous question without acknowledging the need for an answer. A work of art begins as a seed, comes into flower and fertilises the mind-sphere.*

*A format is not a programme.*

1.10    Architects have much to learn from gardening.

2    *WAY OF WORKING*

2.1    In matters where we are ignorant it is best to proceed with caution and not pretend to a knowledge of the nature of artistic creativity and mental process of design which we do not have. Each of us who is a practising artist of any kind has some awareness of how he works, but this is only a partial understanding and we really have no means of knowing what happens in other artists unless they tell us, and this hearsay evidence, based upon incomplete knowledge, is not reliable. Such tests as psychologists can apply may give some light, but you can't investigate creativity very far without changing or even destroying it.

*In this matter psychology has something to learn from physics. The act of observation can alter performance.*

2.2   It would seem to follow that we should not lay down any rules of design but, continuing the garden analogue, we may plan the garden and create conditions in which our plants will grow. We can choose which plants to cultivate but we have to let them do the growing themselves. It may take a long time and we have to be patient.

2.3   In architecture we start with a person, a young man or woman who desires to become an architect. Talent is extremely difficult to diagnose. It cannot be tested by examination, though a reasonable assessment can be made of the student's intellectual capacity to cope with the subjects of study which are currently conventional in the curriculum. This is realistic in relation to things as they happen to be in architectural education and practice.

*Architectural education.*

*Conventions vary and are unstable. It would seem unwise to base architectural education upon localised and ephemeral conditions of practice. (In this context* local *means* national*).*

2.4   The traditional way of educating designers was to work in an office as a pupil/assistant to a master. Guilds of artists conducted trade tests and acclaimed the new graduate with due ceremonial, allowing him to proceed through less supervised experience to eventual mastership. Such a process had its advantages and disadvantages. It tended to be rigorous and restrictive of talent without influence; indeed it was about as exclusive a closed shop as the nobility, and proudly conservative. Academic education had already begun in the medieval monasteries but became organised and secular in France in the seventeenth century. Modern schools of architecture are a development from the *Beaux Arts* system and, perhaps even more importantly, from the educational movements of the mid-nineteenth century which were fuelled by the demand of industry and com-

*Academic education in architecture came late to the educational scene.*

merce for skilled, literate and numerate workers on an unprecedented scale. Pupillage could no longer cope and fell into disrepute. The schools of architecture remain under pressure to produce competent operatives and they have attempted, in various ways, to satisfy the demand, mainly by the dubious process of cultivating an illusion of realism in imaginary projects that will never be built. At the same time they have tried to see beyond the need for operatives and to foster the emergence of artists who will be capable of creating architecture.

*A comparison with history must suggest that present systems, based mainly upon expediency, have failed.*

2.5 Much difficulty arises from a popular myth about art and artists which was propagated in the mid-nineteenth century when old systems of patronage were failing and society was battered by the emergence of industrialism. According to this myth the artist is a lone genius who expresses himself in art, the public response to which is inversely proportional to its merit. This is rubbish!

2.6 The great artists of the past have been hard-working, busy people, often with a shrewd eye for business. Some have worked alone, usually of necessity if, for example, they were topographical painters such as Turner.

2.7 The ideal ambience for an artist is a busy studio with plenty to do and a friendly atmosphere of encouragement and informed criticism. This was and still is achieved in the best architects' offices. A famous example which nurtured several men of genius was that of Richard Norman Shaw in London. Shaw gave opportunity and encouragement. These are the two most important things in architectural education: *the opportunity to explore architecture and the encouragement to do so.*

*The essentials of architectural education.*

2.8 It is foolish and damaging to clutter creative minds with mouldering information. The designer needs to know a few things, according to the nature of his particular design trade (about the main processes and possibilities of printing, for example, if he is a graphic artist). Stored information is nearly always unreliable as well as inhibiting. What the designer needs to be able to do is *find out the best available information at the time of designing.* He needs to learn the technique of finding out and he needs to cultivate standards of judgment and integrity in finding out. If he finds out afresh, rather than drawing upon stored knowledge in his head, the information becomes a new, untarnished stimulus to the design activity.

2.9 There is a ready-made pattern of finding out. It is the standard technique of academic scholarship in any subject and as a technique is applicable to architecture.

*The technique of finding out needs to be learned. We have to learn the meaning of intellectual integrity. This implies an understanding of the limits of knowledge and an enquiring attitude towards phenomena which lie beyond cognition.*

2.10 Integrity and standards of judgment in a designer do not follow automatically from personal integrity.

2.11 The technique of scholarship is developed in universities which do offer one of the two poles between which integrity of judgment in design matters may be achieved. In design we seek excellence, not mediocrity. The same is true of scholarship: this is the academic ideal and basically it is what universities are about; integrity in the pursuit of truth. Much that is done in universities, especially at the administrative level, is distinguishable from this ideal, but the true reason for universities, and it has paid an enormous dividend, is to fulfil the ideal of academic scholarship in the pursuit of wisdom based upon true knowledge in so far as this is attainable—and the boundary moves forward all the time. Architecture needs this kind of integrity and the knowledge and understanding which can be based upon it. It is most necessary in weighing the evidence of sociologists, economists and engineers but also in forming our standards of architectural judgment based upon the truth about the past, and not upon blind prejudices such as prevailed in the renaissance period and in the propagandist phase of the 'modern movement'.

*Architectural education needs to be an intellectual discipline. Merely to experience architecture is not enough.*

2.12 The other basis of excellence is craftsmanship. This is just as relevant in a machine age as in earlier times if only because all machine-made products stem from hand-made prototypes and many machines are in fact elaborate hand tools. Assembly of building components requires craft techniques and the attitudes acquired by a good craftsman in handling materials are of importance to the designer.

*All mass-production starts with the hand-made proto-type.*

2.13 Architectural designers have a craft of their own which is the making of drawings by which they communicate their designs to the executants. This is the first skill to be learned and is perhaps the surest foundation for architectural education, because skill in presenting a design, *truthfully* to oneself as well as to the client and the builder, is the necessary craft of the designer. It is impossible for most people to design well unless they can externalise the design effectively.

2.14 Once the architectural draughtsman's own trade skill has been mastered there is much to be said for the study and acquisition of other relevant skills, as the Bauhaus system advocated. But unless you have at least one highly developed skill as an executant it is probably not much use looking at the way other people work. You tend to miss the point and fail to respect the achievement of the skilled craftsman. It is foolish to think that craft skills can be acquired easily and quickly. For comparison, the kind of understanding which would be acquired by playing the violin once a week 'for a whole year' would be no more than a recognition of the difficulties of making the violin sing in tune, never mind make music!

*Craft skills.*

2.15 Every craft has its special skills and all arts are based upon some degree of craftsmanship. Poor craftsmanship may not inhibit artistic achievement but it certainly restricts it and too often maims it.

*In this matter the visual arts in the twentieth century are far behind music.*

2.16 The advantage for the architect of doing something badly depends upon his personality. In a reasonable person it might be expected to lead to humility and respect, but this is not always so.

## 3 THE LIMITS OF DESIGN

3.1 In most design trades the limit between design and execution is clear.

In popular belief, overwhelmed by the notion that an artist is a painter, the artist is supposed to make the artifact with his own hands. A picture is expected to be the authentic work of the artist except for the canvas or board on which it is painted and the frame which is finally put round it when the work of art is already complete. But with sculpture a doubt arises. Ideally the sculptor works in stone and chips and polishes it all himself, but often he works in clay or plaster and the mould goes to a foundry to be cast in bronze. The finished work of art does not come direct from the hand of the sculptor. Sometimes it does, sometimes it doesn't.

3.2 The architect can hardly ever be the executant of his design and of all art forms his is the most expensive to produce. Somewhere along the line a division has to be made between design and execution. The design itself is often team work: the building always is.

3.3 Two more things seem to be essential for the production of good architecture, the ninth and tenth conditions.

(a) *That the designer carry his part of the work only so far as is compatible with his remaining effective as an artist.*

(b) *That the builder and others involved in execution of the design admire and commit themselves to its realisation.* This sounds simple but is difficult to achieve. In a theory, however, it is appropriate to set standards which are difficult to fulfil, particularly when there is evidence that they can be fulfilled.

*The ninth and tenth conditions of architecture.*

*As for example in Gothic church architecture.*

3.4 The achievement of good architecture depends upon the collaboration of all the people involved in design, finance, administration and building. This cannot be achieved by the architect alone and the client has an indispensable role. It might seem that the architect is the person who has to bring all the parties into effective collaboration. This is the assumption in professional practice in many countries. Its weakness is that it exonerates the client, and this is probably the main reason why it does not work.

*But if the tenth condition is to be fulfilled there would seem to be an obligation upon the architect to be concerned with job-satisfaction throughout the building team. Most architects think they have a right, as artists, to job-satisfaction, indeed this is a fetish and many would say it is impossible to design well without it, but it does not stop there.*

3.5 Whatever the organisation and division of responsibility, the designer cannot work alone. He is part of a consortium but his special role is to design the architecture. Nobody else has this responsibility.

3.6 There are and have been many different systems for getting a design built. Putting the architect in complete charge is profitable to the architect professionally, but there is little or no evidence that it is the best way of producing good architecture.

3.7 The architect is a designer. Only as a designer can he be identified as an architect.

# 4 ARTISTIC TECHNIQUE

All art rests upon a foundation of technique. Technique is the ability to do what you want to do.

4.1 But what do we want to do? Just as the painter does not copy onto canvas a vision which is complete in his own mind, so the architect works by the interpretation of feed-back from what he has already done. *It is a process of continuous creation from an initial stimulus, the brief, through a series of stimuli to a final design.*

*Continuous challenge and response.*

4.2 An architect cannot design an unspecified building on an undefined site. If he were asked to do this he would begin with assumptions. On the basis of assumptions he could design architecture. Some of the seminal ideas in architecture have been developed in designs which were never built. The books of Palladio and Serlio, which were greatly influential in seventeenth and eighteenth-century architecture, contain designs which those architects never built themselves and for which they had only hypothetical clients and notional sites. Much of the architecture of the eastern states of the USA in the eighteenth century stemmed from such books published in England, especially James Gibbs' *Book of Architecture*.

*Hypothetical architecture for a hypothetical client is a valuable exercise and means of exploration but real architecture must have a real client. This actually happened in the execution of some of Palladio's hypothetical designs for real clients in eighteenth century England.*

4.3 From the Gothic age we have evidence of notional schemes. From the Gothic Revival we have innumerable examples of ideal designs for which there was only a notional client.

4.4 The consummation of architectural design is actual building, just as the consummation of a novel is printing and publishing. These are honourable trades with their own techniques and a strong element of design but the art of the novelist is in writing: likewise the art of the architect is in designing. His fundamental technique is in communicating his design to those who are going to build—the client, the financiers, the builder, the sub-contractors, the craftsmen and workmen—but the design is the architect's contribution.

*The professional architect as defined, for example, in the British Architects Registration Act, is trying and claiming to be much more than an architect in the proper sense of that word.*

4.5 How much does the architect need to know about building? The answer to this depends upon the organisation and efficiency of the building industry.

4.6 The ideal would seem to be that the architect knows enough about building to choose or agree to a suitable way (format) of building, to understand how the chosen way works and exploit its possibilities reasonably and efficiently. He must make a design and communicate that design to the executants just as an author presents an intelligible typescript or a composer a legible and playable musical score.

*Much of the best architecture has resulted from the adoption of a simple and limiting format. Many architects make things much more difficult for themselves than is necessary. There is no virtue in virtuosity deployed in the solution of problems which need never have arisen!*

4.7 Someone has to see that the architect's design is carried out. This may involve consultation from time to time, because no communication is infallible, but the responsibility for execution is distinct from that of designing. This has always been understood but there is a current dogma in some countries that the architect should be responsible for the execution of his design. In an ideal world this might be possible. In the world as it is the architect needs the back-up of an efficient and conscientious client and builder. It is impossible to have good architecture if the client does not accept responsibility for the final product.

*The essential role and responsibility of the client.*

4.8 Architecture is often said to reflect society. It does, and there is nothing architects can do about it, as architects, except to offer the best of which they are capable. *The responsibility for architecture rests upon the people in a society who commission buildings.*

4.9 It follows that architectural education should extend to clients. They are an essential part of the building process. The architect's role is to design as best he can.

*This does not mean that the architect should dictate to the client what he ought to like: it implies a genuine partnership. This is the only basis for a humane architecture. Some schools of architecture are moving towards this.*

## 5 HOW CAN HE BEST DESIGN?

5.1 Everything that has been done in the whole of history is only a glimpse of a tiny part of what might be done. None of the great periods of architecture was entirely logical: each was a natural growth of astonishing originality. It was original, not because anybody made it so but because it was the unselfconscious work of creative minds.

5.2 Creativity is important. Originality is a consequence not an intention. It is extremely unoriginal to strive to be original. Originality has to *happen*.

5.3 The starting point is people. What do they want and

*The basis of the partnership referred to above.*

what will they enjoy? Coincident with starting is the architect's suppression of himself. He must surrender to his subject, his programme, his people.

5.4 The architect who despises people and considers himself or herself superior to people should give up and get a job as a prison warder.

5.5 The architect should know the full range of available possibilities in architecture. These are the *formats*. The format should be chosen and 'explained to the people. They should have the chance to reject it and choose another format.

**Know** *in the sense of* be aware of, *not necessarily practise. It is probably impossible to practise effectively in more than a very few formats.*

5.6 An architect may very well reject a particular format because he is out of sympathy with it and therefore incapable of working effectively in that particular format. Or the architect may plead ignorance and would be morally right to do so if he is unable to provide a proper service within the preferred format. But we must avoid the idea that any format is itself immoral.

5.7 Let us face the implications of this. It is not immoral for an architect to design in any format provided that he is competent to do so. It is plain bad trading for an architect to design in a format in which he is not competent. If a brewery decides to build a public house in the Cotswold style it is entitled, as a part of our contemporary society, to do so. An architect may rightly say he does not work in that style, but any architect who takes on the job should do it as well as possible. This is what makes the consensus of an age in architecture; not the prejudices of a self-appointed and censorious élite but what people actually want, and the architect's job is to give them what they want to the best of his design ability. Otherwise the whole concept of culture is a fraud, or an attempted fraud, because in fact any age has to be looked at by historians for what it *really* was.

*The Cotswolds are a range of hills in the West of England with a characteristic vernacular format.*

5.8 History is important for architects because it provides a case-history of experiments, but if they try to influence history it is a different matter. The important thing is to live in one's own time as an architect and as a designer.

5.9 Anything else is a deceit.

# 6    THE AVAILABLE FORMATS

6.1    A client may decide to build a tobacco factory in a style derived from Turkish mosques of the seventeenth century. There are innumerable examples to show that it is not an offensive or ugly style. In some strange way the decision reflects the character of the age.

6.2    A client decides to erect a modern sky-scraper hotel overlooking the grounds of a royal palace. There is an ethical question of seemliness reflecting the client's attitude to royalty and the community in which the building is to be placed socially. Likewise a developer wants to erect a high building adjoining St Paul's Cathedral in London or St Basil in Moscow. The format in both cases is being imposed by the client and the town-planning ethics should operate, not against the architect, but in order to ensure that the format is seemly for society. The concept of right format is essential to good planning. But for architects there is a sequence of problems. First, 'Do I approve of the format in the circumstances?' Second, 'Can I design in this format? Do I have the requisite training and knowledge?' Third, 'Is this a way of design in which I can give of my best?'

*Here 'modern' is used in a stylistic sense.*

**The arrogant client is more common than the arrogant architect.**

6.3    None of these questions is a moral question about a kind of architecture. All of them are moral questions to the artist about his fitness to *start* designing, his fitness to accept the commission.

6.4    Once again we must insist upon a clear intellectual distinction being made between what is an ethical decision and what is an aesthetic decision. Ethically the architect is a man or woman: aesthetically he or she is an artist. The role of the artist who has accepted a format is to design as well as possible within that format.

6.5    Acceptance of a format greatly simplifies design, limits the field in which decisions have to be made and enables the architect to concentrate all his talents upon a particular way of design.

6.6    Antique formats are generally clearly defined. A need arises for the definition, in all their aspects, of modern formats.

6.7 Every architect has to discover the formats in which he can work. Definition of the formats can help him. Often this process is called 'a personal philosophy' but it is no such thing, It is no more a philosophy than the choosing by a poet to write in blank verse or the choosing by a painter to be a miniaturist. It is a simple but very important matter of finding congenial formats. In criticism a clear distinction should be made between comment on the format as such and comment on the performance of the architect. This is well understood in criticism of most of the other arts. One may say of a literary work that it might have been more appropriately handled as a novel than as a play. This is a criticism of choice of format. Normally it will affect judgment of the play but the distinction has been made.

*A note on architectural criticism.*

6.8 A theory of architecture should not and cannot define or explain all the formats, any more than a theory of painting can explain how to paint in oils or water-colour or a theory of music discuss the techniques of orchestration.

6.9 It is the job of the schools of architecture to teach and explore formats.

*As things are at present the only form of teaching would be exploration. Joint exploration by teacher and pupil is probably the best form of teaching anyway.*

6.10 Quality in architecture is likely to be achieved by the refinement of formats. Following an experimental period such as the 'modern movement' has been, there seems to be a need for refinement, the selection of successful prototypes and the rejection of failures, particularly in the use of materials and structural forms.

*This emphasises the importance of studying architecture. Learning by designing is not enough and the current vogue for project-related teaching needs to be questioned.*

6.11 But no format is final, not even the historical formats. It has often been shown that the use of an historical format by a creative designer has developed the format. Modern formats, ill-defined though they still are, already show the effects of changing fashion.

*High-rise housing is a format which is failing to stand the test of experience.*

6.12 Fashion reflects the needs and condition of people. It is a phenomenon. There is no one architecture for ever and ever. But are there any constants in design?

*Variety is essential for freedom. Uniformity is bondage.*

7    DESIGN CONSTANTS

7.1 Architecture began with man giving significance to building.

7.2    There is always the duality of *building* and *significance*. Architecture is never simply significant of itself unless, very rarely, a man decides to try and make it so, but this is a human decision and the building becomes a reflection of human will, inevitably.

7.3    In this context 'truthful expression' which has preoccupied the minds of architects recently, can only be a *balance* between a function and humane significance.

7.4    Form can only follow function where a single function can be isolated. This cannot happen in architecture because it is always bi-polar—humane significance and functional building—even in the most simple example. Most buildings are multi-functional and highly complex. The architect can select functional or structural elements for expression or suppression, but people come before purposes and the humane significance of the building is most important.

7.5    The first balance is between people and site. If all buildings were designed by architects and all architects were perfect, town-planners would be able to concentrate on town-planning. Architect or architect-and-planner must balance the client's desires against environmental considerations, the interest of the community (which is the external client), and the interests of the inhabitants (represented by the client), which is the real internal client.

7.6    The format of the building is agreed among the interested parties. This is the starting-point of the architectural design.

7.7    The specification of the format must include the external materials. A competent architect must be able to design in any material finish which is required, and agreed.

*It is not a matter of whim or of conscience. The choice of materials is of concern to many people besides the architect.*

7.8    On any site where there are adjoining buildings the scale and character are indicated.

7.9    Departure from existing scale or materials needs to be justified on the ground that the locality will be improved by the discrepancy.

7.10    After the format comes the programme. This needs

to be a collaborative effort of the client and architect, the client explaining his need and intentions, the architect already beginning to make a design contribution by interpreting the client's instructions in the light of architectural knowledge. A difficulty arises in making some clients understand that this is an essential part of the design activity and it cannot be achieved satisfactorily unless there is a proper client. By *proper client* we mean a person, or group, with knowledge and authority to make decisions which, collaboratively with the architect, are design decisions. Much bad architecture results, despite architects, from client failure. Good architecture requires confidence and collaboration between architect and client. The client must really exist for the design process to work. This is why so much government-sponsored architecture is bad: there is no real client.

*Design by students in a school of architecture has to be a simulation of real architectural design. It is an exercise, a means of exploration like the hypothetical design referred to above. The introduction of a 'client' does not alter this because he is not a real client. Being an illusion he is liable to mislead.*

7.11   When the programme has been designed within the agreed format the architect can begin his real job of designing the building in relation to its environment.

7.12   Design is a creative process in which all the final syntheses are made in the mind of a designer. This is equally true for individual and group work but in the latter case there is a process of consensus (feeling together) leading through continuous intercommunication to a design synthesis in one of the minds and collective agreement with that synthesis. Psychologically the process is complicated and could perhaps be much better understood; but to designers it is familiar and workable, so it is questionable whether any practical advantage would result from academic psychological analysis, though this might be beneficial in other directions.

*It is necessary to say that the student in a school of architecture is involved in a real learning process but only in a simulated design process. This needs to be accepted; learning to design then becomes a reality distinct from actual designing. Much bad modern architecture has been produced as a result of boom conditions which have allowed what are in fact no more than design exercises actually to be built. So we have vast structures which look like final-year thesis designs, not real architecture.*

7.13   The artistic faculty of the human mind is procreative. The designer is not making something out of something: he is creating anew. It is therefore impossible to foreknow a design just as it is impossible to foreknow the character of an unborn child. There are many quack nostrums called 'design processes' (which may be compared with vaginal douches of Nile water in the physical process of procreation). We know even less about mental creativity than we do about physical reproduction, which in fact among human beings is never reproduction and always new creation. Given a chance the mind of an artist will work to create architecture.

7.14 Design is not a process: it is an intuition but it is well known in western art and eastern philosophy that the powers of the mind to intuit can be cultivated. This is the true meaning of the word education.

*The cultivation of intuition by discipline and study.*

7.15 It follows that our Theory of Architecture will not conclude with some rules for designing but with an encouragement of all those who aspire to be architects to study and contemplate, by whatever disciplines may be suitable, the phenomenon of architecture in all its manifestations as a product of the creative power of mind.

7.16 The way of being an architect is only open to those with creative minds of a special kind. Such people are precious and should not be wasted. They need and deserve the support of many others skilled in the business of building who may well study this book to understand what it is they are about. But the endowment of artistic talent is not enough. Architecture is only one in the sense that it is recognisable, independently of time, place and style. The experience, study and creative contemplation of all architecture is the discipline of architectural education. Thereafter a man or woman may *begin* to be fit to serve mankind as an architect.

APPENDIX

A Note on Functionalism and Common Sense.

Functionalism has had an important influence upon modern
architecture and upon architectural education but the
foundations of functionalism are even more spurious than
those of classical aesthetic theory.   From classical
theory functionalism accepts absolutely, that beauty is
a property of things.   It adds the notion that fitness
for purpose is the determinant of beauty.   As an aesthetic
theory, even if we accept the objectivity of beauty this is
a nonsense.   Beauty is not dependent upon whether a thing
works or not and as I argued in *Art and the Nature of
Architecture* (London 1952) beautiful objects, such as
microscopes which are functionally designed do not cease
to be beautiful if there is an invisible internal fault
which renders them useless.   Likewise a Rolls Royce
*Silver Ghost* is just as beautiful to the beholder if the
gear-box has been removed or even the engine.   It seems
silly to argue that a thing is beautiful if it has been
designed to work well even if it does not.   The mistake
lies in confusing beauty of appearance, which is an
aesthetic matter, with performance which is a utilitarian
matter.   According to functionalism any cheap modern
motor vehicle is more beautiful than *The Silver Ghost*.
      Another aspect of functionalism is linked to ethics
rather than aesthetics.   There is a belief that things
*ought* to be designed purely in terms of their function.
A nineteenth century steam tractor with its ornamental
canopy and decorative embellishments which many people
think are charming is 'wrong'.   I think this kind of
puritanism is very tedious and will leave it at that.
      As might be expected, a theory or doctrine which is
based upon fallacies leads to misunderstandings and
mistakes.   Obviously there is sense in designing things
so that they work well:   the mistake was to elevate plain
common sense into an aesthetic and to some extent an
ethical doctrine.   The result has too often been to
obscure the virtues of common sense and I would suggest
that architecture would be improved, and made more humane,
if we were to forget about functionalism and simply keep
asking ourselves, in the process or designing, 'What is.
the *sensible* thing to do?'
      As an example let us consider for a moment the design
of windows.   These are necessary in most buildings.
From a common sense point of view they are commonly very
badly designed and are among the worst features of

modernistic architecture.   As· an extreme example consider
a suite of teaching rooms in a university with a continuous
window so that there is only glass against which to stop
the partitions between the rooms.   Or consider a south-
facing office building, with glass from floor to ceiling
and wall to wall, in which an acceptable degree of comfort
can only be achieved by having screens and blinds.   Too
often the windows on the north side of a building (in the
northern hemisphere) are just the same as the windows on
the south side - for 'architectural' reasons.   This is
plain idiocy but if we take the functionalist point of
view seriously and accept the simple statement that the
purpose of a window is to let in day-light and the more
it does that the better it is, we can justify that idiocy
though we may discredit architects in the eyes of sensible
people.   In fact the diagnosis was wrong;  the function
of a window is not only to let in light.   Everything in
a building is a compromise.

If on the other hand we start with people and ask
what kind of window they would most like to have we are
initially frustrated by the fact that most people now
assume they will have to put up with what the architect
decides to give them and they don't really know what is
possible.   This is where sympathy and empathy come in.
What kind of window would really be best in an apartment
block?   Certainly not a flat slab of glass in a flat
facade - probably a bay window which adds further floor
space, amplifies the outlook, and ideally that bay window
would have top light for the benefit of pot plants and
internal window boxes.   Not everybody wants to grow
plants in their windows you may say, but take a look
around:  most people do if they can, and healthy growing
plants are a source of pleasure.   Why not provide for
them?.

If architecture is to be humane rather than doctrin-
aire sympathetic common sense should replace functionalism.

Finally there are those who think that the cheapest
solution is the best.   This is a perverted kind of
functionalism which gives top priority to saving money.
Again common sense should be substituted and common sense
is related to a sense of proportion.

POSTSCRIPT

For many years I have been discussing, thinking and writing
about the theory of architecture.   The discipline of
writing has been an essential part of my thinking process
and now, from a great deal of material, I have tried to
crystalise a systematic statement.   Much of it is old and
has been known to architects, off and on, through the
centuries:   some of it derives from the modern movement
which was a significant turn in the history of architecture:   some things are seen in a new light and perhaps
there are a few original thoughts.   I confess that it has
been very difficult to compile this book in a way which is I
hope concise and intelligible without being simplistic.
The aim has been to dissolve the shackles of dogma and open
up the subject of architecture to creative study and specu-
lation.   The form is a mosaic not a linear argument and I
hope it may create a multi-dimensional mosaic of understanding.

     Now that I have done what I can and the book is
complete I am tempted to make a few comments of my own in
advance of criticism.   These are topical and perhaps
ephemeral.   If my work proves to have any lasting value
they may become irrelevant and be excluded from future
editions but it is commonly thought that we are at a time
of change in the development of architecture and having
done my job in an ambience of architectural education,
practice and artistic creativity, from which experience I
have derived stimulus and inspiration, I want to feed-back
from what I have done, to the situation in which my work
was generated, by commenting on its implications for
practice and education.

     There will be some worthy people of the old school
who will see in what I have written a justification for
reaction, for a return to things as they were before the
modern movement.   I wish them joy of any comfort they
may have but I am not on their side though I do believe
some of them have knowledge which is no longer easy to
come by.

     The modern movement was not in vain:   it was a
tremendous achievement the substantial values of which
should not be squandered.   It came as a necessary correc-
tive to stylistic eclecticism which was a great idea for
the nineteenth century when it really seemed that western
civilization, and especially the British and French Empires,
were a consummation of all preceeding civilizations so
that a stylistic synthesis of all that had ever been
achieved in architecture was right and proper.

The modern movement coincided with a new vision but it was also affected by totalitarianism. Greed, intolerance, rigidity and the old barbarian ambitions to dominate found their reflection in a world-wide manifestation of architecture which is, in fact, a denial of most of the original ideas which inspired the modern movement. In this context the need is for liberation, for an ecumenical approach to architecture which will release the creative genius of designers to work in the contexts of their own communities. Man is one species and we must learn to live in harmony or perish but the way is not through uniformity and the imposition of an ideology. The surface of Earth provides innumerable different environments and is enriched by a great variety of human traditions. The concept of architectural formats is seen by me as a way of releasing creativity as well as preserving our inheritance.

A format is not a style though a style may be a format. A format is not arbitrary and to be adopted by the whim of architect or client. It is to be seen as a design discipline which is provenly suitable for people and climate. The nature of *suitability* has been a main theme of this book and I will not go over the ground again but I want to say a little more about the nature and implications of architectural format.

Architecture is made by people and people have to learn to be architects. In the nineteenth century they learned to design in styles and studied the appropriate methods of construction. Early in the twentieth century schools of architecture began to flourish and there was a revival of classical principles. Established classicism which did in effect teach a single, well-tried format, was the basis for an easy transition to crypto-classical modernism, but the modern idiom has failed to develop the necessary internal disciplines of a format for reasons which have been indicated. Modernism became a style with its own characteristic features, derived very largely from fashion and the proliferation of imitation rather than from any deeply studied discipline, functional or otherwise.

It was probably inevitable that a world-wide mode of design which deliberately rejected local influences, even to the extent of ignoring climate in many cases, became too generalised to be a format because a format must, of its nature, be particular and limited. This is its great advantage as a vehicle for designing. The result, in education, has been that in most schools students are not taught to design and in a sense it is actually true that they do not know how to design; nor do many of

their tutors.    Design is supposed to come from the nature
of the problem simply by working on it.    In a succession
of projects students are supposed to acquire and develop
an ability to design out of themselves.    This makes
criticism and teaching very difficult to the point where
quality of design is a matter of opinion, some opinions
being 'more equal than others' to borrow Orwell's famous
phrase.

*A distinction could be made between being able to design and knowing how to design*

*It may be thought that many practising architects can design but it is reasonable to expect a teacher to know how to design.*

But *how to design* can be seen as being like how to
play tennis, how to ski or how to cultivate a vegetable
garden.    In cultivating a garden at least there are
established methods, formats, which vary from place to
place according to soil and climate and what we want to
grow, from artichokes to zucchini.

I have suggested that we need to develop architectural formats which are appropriate to people and places.
To do this we must abandon most of the methods now
conventionally used in schools of architecture and begin
by recognising two fundamental facts:  firstly students
come from various places, in most schools from many
countries, climates and cultural backgrounds:  secondly
they will be dispersed to many different places when they
graduate.

If we ditch the concept of a single world style, which
we must do, we must learn to explore and design in various
formats.  Exploration must precede design and the dogma of
learning by designing has to be questioned.    The abomina-
tion of forty or fifty students in one big studio all
ignorantly designing the same building in the modern idiom
must go.    It is not a good way of learning to design, as
the built results plainly show.

But the formats are not ready-made.    We cannot
suddenly switch over to designing in formats.    These have
to be studied, explored, formulated, tried out, modified
and kept flexible.    This means that the next stage in
architectural education must be based upon exploration
and study by staff as much as students in an atmosphere of
discovery.    But more than zeal is required:  knowledge of
formats will not happen by accident in an aura of
enthusiasm!

It is necessary to isolate and state the problem
clearly so that it can be studied scientifically.    A
format is a way of designing buildings within convenient
and suitable limits.    A model exists in the classical
system of design.    As we have seen the underlying dogma
may be corrupt but there is a sense in which all human
building, indeed all human knowledge rests upon unsure
foundations.    We can recognise classical design as a

format.    We can study its origins, principles, discipline, exemplification, the way it works and its many sub-formats. Likewise we can study Gothic church architecture without necessarily sharing the beliefs of thirteenth century Christian theologians, or Islamic mosques without being Mohammedans.    Every kind of architecture can be *investigated* in order to understand what was achieved architectonically and how it was achieved.    The Palace of Minos had architectonic values which, in some respects, can put Palladio or Le Corbusier to shame.    But this is going a long way back and all over the surface of Earth there are ways of building, rooted in the soil, in the climate, materials and culture of peoples, which can be identified and studied as formats

But let us be careful.    The last thing we want is *A History of Formats on the Comparative Method* rivalling Banister-Fletcher's famous history of architectural styles.

The reason for studying format is to provide a way of studying architecture and I believe it is necessary to bring more study of architecture into architectural education.    Opinions may differ about the desirability of actually designing in an antique format.    Personally I would not wish to encourage pastiche as a mode of design. But the study of formats is not a design activity:   it is an investigation of architecture and architecture can be recognised as an entire phenomenon over the whole history of all mankind.    In studying a format one is aiming to acquire awareness of architecture and a vocabulary for discussing it such as exists in the discussion of literature or mathematics.

At some point, probably coincidently with the study of format, the student must design, for that is what he wants to learn to do.    The choice of a format in which to design has to make sense but I do not think it would be right to lay down any law about this.    Different schools and teachers will need to work out their own best ways of using formats in design and these will depend to quite a large extent upon the location of the school and the actual buildings which are available for study. It may be that certain 'grand formats' such as classicism, will commend themselves for generalised study but I would suggest that the investigation of real architecture in its environment is the best basis.    After all we are not, I hope, trying to resuscitate old ways of design but to learn from what exists how to design in our own age. Where a genuine folk or vernacular architecture exists it can demonstrate fundamentals of design in an environmental context, and it is very valuable study material.

All the formats which exist have come into being and evolved.   The ways in which this has happened are fascinating but that is the subject of another book.   Five factors may be mentioned:  the environment, the culture of the people, their technology, their economy, and the work of creative architects designing within the evolving format. All these are still relevant.   Architecture is still evolving and suddenly we may see in the modern movement the means of its salvation.

Location and creation.   Many modern architects have been aware of the need to relate their work to locations. The great mistake of the modern movement was characteristic of its time:  it sought and claimed to be universal - total: and it put form before people.   It did not and could not produce a single universal format:  for this we should be thankful but all over Earth there are the beginnings of new formats growing out of creative design, in places and for people.

Out of the study of successful ways of designing, the need to localise and the recognition of architectonic values we can move to the evolution of new formats, new ways of designing for people.

A Modern Theory of Architecture

# A MODERN THEORY

# OF

# ARCHITECTURE

BRUCE ALLSOPP

ROUTLEDGE & KEGAN PAUL

LONDON, HENLEY & BOSTON

*First published in 1977*
*by Routledge & Kegan Paul Ltd*
*39 Store Street,*
*London WC1E 7DD,*
*Broadway House,*
*Newtown Road,*
*Henley-on-Thames,*
*Oxon RG9 1EN and*
*9 Park Street,*
*Boston, Mass. 02108, USA*

*Set in Bembo*
*and printed in Great Britain by*
*Knight & Forster Ltd., Leeds*

*ISBN 0 7100 8611 3*